LEADER'S GUIDE

Dr. Justo González, writer of this study resource, was born in Havana, Cuba, the son of two Methodist ministers. He completed his S.T.B. at Union Theological Seminary in Matanzas, Cuba, and then came to the United States to pursue graduate studies in theology. He obtained his Ph.D. in historical theology from Yale University. Since that time, he has held teaching positions at the Evangelical Seminary of Puerto Rico and Candler School of Theology. Although he now teaches on an occasional basis, he is a full-time writer and lecturer.

His books, originally written in either Spanish or English, have been translated into several other languages. He has also written numerous United Methodist curriculum materials as well as materials for other denominations.

ACTS

Copyright © 1995 by Cokesbury
All rights reserved.

JOURNEY THROUGH THE BIBLE: ACTS. LEADER'S GUIDE. An official resource for The United Methodist Church prepared by the General Board of Discipleship through the division of Church School Publications and published by Cokesbury, a division of The United Methodist Publishing House; 201 Eighth Avenue, South; P.O. Box 801; Nashville, TN 37202. Printed in the United States of America. Copyright ©1995 by Cokesbury.

Scripture quotations in this publication, unless otherwise indicated, are from the New Revised Standard Version of the Bible, copyright ©1989 by the Division of Christian Education of the National Council of the Churches of Christ in the United States of America, and are used by permission. All rights reserved.

For permission to reproduce any material in this publication, call 615-749-6421, or write to Cokesbury, Syndication—Permissions Office, P.O. Box 801, Nashville, TN 37202.

To order copies of this publication, call toll free 800-672-1789. Call Monday–Friday 7:30–5:00 Central Time or 8:30–4:30 Pacific Time. Use your Cokesbury account, American Express, Visa, Discover, or MasterCard.

EDITORIAL TEAM

Debra G. Ball-Kilbourne,
Editor

Linda H. Leach,
Assistant Editor

Linda O. Spicer,
Adult Section Assistant

DESIGN TEAM

Ed Wynne,
Layout Designer

Susan J. Scruggs,
Design Supervisor,
Cover Design

ADMINISTRATIVE STAFF

Neil M. Alexander,
Vice-President, Publishing

Duane A. Ewers,
Editor of Church School Publications

Gary L. Ball-Kilbourne,
Executive Editor of Adult Publications

 Cokesbury

06 07 08 09 – 11 10 9 8 7

THIS PUBLICATION IS PRINTED ON RECYCLED PAPER

Contents

Volume 13: Acts ·· by Justo L. González

$\mathcal{I}$NTRODUCTION TO THE SERIES

The leader's guides provided for use with JOURNEY THROUGH THE BIBLE make the following assumptions:

● adults learn in different ways:
  —by reading
  —by listening to speakers
  —by working on projects
  —by drama and roleplay
  —by using their imaginations
  —by expressing themselves creatively
  —by teaching others

● the mix of persons in your group is different from that found in any other group.

● the length of the actual time you have for teaching in a session may vary from thirty minutes to ninety minutes.

● the physical place where your class meets is not exactly like the place where any other group or class meets.

● your teaching skills, experiences, and preferences are unlike anyone else's.

We encourage you to discover and develop the ways you can best use the information and learning ideas in this leader's guide with your particular class. To get started, we suggest you try following these steps:

1. Think and pray about your individual class members. Who are they? What are they like? Why are they involved in this particular Bible study class at this particular time in their lives? What seem to be their needs? How do you think they learn best?

2. Think and pray about your class members as a group. A group takes on a character that can be different from the particular characters of the individuals who make up that group. How do your class members interact? What do they enjoy doing together? What would help them become stronger as a group?

3. Keep in mind that you are teaching this class for the sake of the class members, in order to help them increase in their faithfulness as disciples of Jesus Christ. Teachers sometimes fall prey to the danger of teaching in ways that are easiest for themselves. The best teachers accept the discomfort of taking risks and stretching their teaching skills in order to focus on what will really help the class members learn and grow in their faith.

4. Read the chapter in the study book. Read the assigned Bible passages. Read the background Bible passages, if any. Work through the Dimension 1 questions in the study book. Make a list of any items you do not understand and need to research further using such tools as Bible dictionaries, concordances, Bible atlases, and commentaries. In other words, do your homework. Be prepared with your own knowledge about the Bible passages being studied by your class.

5. Read the chapter's material in the leader's guide. You might want to begin with the "Additional Bible Helps," found at the *end* of each chapter. Then look at each learning idea in the "Learning Menu."

6. Spend some time with the "Learning Menu." Notice that the "Learning Menu" is organized around Dimensions 1, 2, and 3 in the study book. Recognizing that different adults and adult classes will learn best using different teaching/learning methods, in each of the three dimensions you will find
  —at least one learning idea that is primarily discussion-based;
  —at least one learning idea that begins with a method other than discussion, but which may lead into discussion.
  Make notes about which learning ideas will work best given the unique makeup and setting of your class.

7. Decide on a lesson plan. Which learning ideas will you lead the class members through when? What materials will you need? What other preparations do you need to make? How long do you plan to spend on a particular learning idea?

8. Many experienced teachers have found that they do better if they plan more than they actually use during a class session. They also know that their class members may become frustrated if they try to do too much during a class session. In other words
  —plan more than you can actually use. That way, you have back-up learning ideas in case something does not work well or something takes much less time than you thought.
  —don't try to do everything listed in the "Learning Menu." We have intentionally offered you much more than you can use in one class session.
  —be flexible while you teach. A good lesson plan is only a guide for your use as you teach people. Keep the focus on your class members, not your lesson plan.

9. After you teach, evaluate the class session. What worked well? What did not? What did you learn from your experience of teaching that will help you plan for the next class session?

May God's Spirit be upon you as you lead your class on their *Journey Through the Bible*!

1

Acts 2:1-13

TONGUES

LEARNING MENU

Keeping in mind the ways in which your class members learn best, as well as their needs and interests, choose at least one learning segment from each of the three Dimensions that follow. Remember that Dimension 1 activities explore what the Bible says and put biblical events into a larger geographical and historical context. Dimension 2 activities explore what Jesus meant according to the writer of the Acts of the Apostles and how Luke's original audience heard it. Dimension 3 activities explore what the passages mean in students' personal lives, congregational lives, and lives as disciples in God's world.

Acts of the Apostles highlights the role of the Holy Spirit in the lives of early Christians. Prayer vividly connects us with the Holy Spirit. Therefore, each session includes an opening prayer. Use these prayers as part of your personal meditation and preparation to teach. Adapt them for use in your class.

Opening Prayer

Almighty God,
you poured your Spirit upon gathered disciples
creating bold tongues, open ears,
and a new community of faith.
We confess that we hold back the force of your Spirit
among us.
We do not listen for your word of grace,
speak the good news of your love,
or live as a people made one in Christ.

Have mercy on us, O God.
Transform our timid lives by the power of your Spirit,
and fill us with a flaming desire to be your faithful
people,
doing your will for the sake of Jesus Christ our Lord.
Amen.

(From *Book of Common Worship.* ©1993 Westminster/John Knox Press)

Dimension 1: What Does the Bible Say?

(A) Review questions in the study book.

- The answers to Dimension 1 questions can be discovered by reading Acts 2:1-13.
- The purpose of the Dimension 1 questions listed on page 4 of the study book is to encourage participants to read the text carefully before the class session and to begin highlighting some of the points that will be important in the session itself.
- Encourage participants to read their Bibles before each future session, looking for answers to the Dimension 1 questions.
- Since this is the first session of the study, give students time when they arrive to read the passage and write out answers to the questions.
- Review the sequence of the story and the answers to the questions with the class.

(B) Share images of Pentecost.

- Provide newsprint and markers.
- Assign students the task of working in small discussion groups of three to five members.
- Ask discussion groups to use materials provided to identify images that come to mind when they think about Pentecost. (This might include the first Christian Pentecost or current Pentecosts, since Pentecost is increasingly becoming a much celebrated holy day in Christian churches.) Groups may want to document the different feelings they discover regarding Pentecost, recording these feelings on newsprint using words or sketches.

(C) Sing about Pentecost.

- Use your congregation's hymnal.
- Sing hymns related to Pentecost or the Holy Spirit.
- Ask:
—What do the hymns of our faith say about the Holy Spirit?
—What do the hymns of our faith say about Pentecost?
—How closely do the texts of the hymns capture the Scripture for today's session?
- Using chalk and chalkboard or newsprint and markers, record the responses of participants. Post responses where class members can easily see them during the session.

(D) Read the text dramatically.

- Turn to Acts 2:1-13 or reproduce copies of the passage.
- Enlist the help of participants to share the text aloud. You will need a narrator and the crowds.
- If you wish, ask a participant to read the part of Peter and continue to read through the rest of chapter 2.

Dimension 2: What Does the Bible Mean?

(E) Make three points.

- In Dimension 2 activities the following three points should be underscored. The context in which Luke was written and the challenges to which it responds are threefold:
  1. Roman authorities who were suspicious of Christians
  2. Jewish Christians who looked askance at Gentile Christianity
  3. Christians who faced trials and difficulties because of their faith
- Draw a triangle as follows:

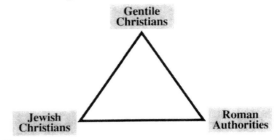

- Share:
—Luke was probably a Gentile Christian. If he was Jewish in background, he certainly was in favor of the mission to the Gentiles and the church that was resulting from it.
- Place Luke's name just below "Gentile Christians."
- Ask:
—If you were Luke, what would you try to tell each of these groups?
- Begin with the Gentile Christians.
—Share that Gentile Christians were true believers, and that the Gentile church was the result of the work and guidance of the Holy Spirit rather than something strange that someone invented.
- Move to the Roman authorities.
—Share that Christianity was not subversive, and that Christians had traditionally obeyed the authorities. Christians likewise had traditionally respected authorities. Christians also showed integrity when dealing with corrupt government agents.
- Finally, turn to Jewish Christians.
—Share that from the beginning the Holy Spirit was working to create a church that was wider than the original

community. Some within the original community had the same misgivings that present Jewish Christians have. Many, however, were eventually convinced by the witness of the Holy Spirit.

- Ask the class to remember the three groupings and to look for evidence of these things as they read and study the rest of the book.

Optional Method

Choose this option only if you can do so well in advance of the class session, giving participants ample time to think about their assignment.

- Since you probably have participants in your class who have read Acts before, and some who may know it quite well, you may select three such persons. Assign to each of them one of the three "directions" in which Luke must have been looking as he wrote Acts.
- Ask each person to try to find a passage in which Luke seemed to be dealing with that concern; then ask persons to bring a very brief report to the study session. (The purpose is not to study the passage they suggest, but rather to whet the appetite of the entire class for this sort of reading, where one tries to see what particular agendas or concerns the author had.)
- At the end of the presentation of this point, no matter which option you have chosen, challenge the class, as they read Acts during the next three months, to look for Luke's treatment of these issues.
- Those present at the beginning of the events of Pentecost probably were not only the Twelve but the entire Christian community.

(F) Look at illustrations.

- Invite students to view the two illustrations depicting Pentecost in the study book, pages 6-7.
- Ask:
—On the basis of the readings from Acts, which of these two illustrations seems to be closer to what Acts says? (Make it clear that you are talking about the composition of the group, and not such items as their clothing, the physical setting, and such other secondary matters.)
- Invite people to look at the entire narrative in Acts 1 and 2 for hints as to how to respond to that question.
—Possible arguments in favor of only the Twelve: (1) Acts 2:14 says that "Peter, standing up with the eleven . . . ." (2) Immediately before Pentecost, the eleven elected Matthias to be the twelfth apostle. Thus, the "all" following that action would seem to mean all twelve.

—Possible arguments in favor of more than the Twelve: (1) In the election of Matthias, Luke expressly told us that the group involved in that election was much larger than the eleven—closer to one hundred and twenty people. (2) Just before in Acts 1:14 Luke told us that those who were constantly gathering for prayer included, not only the Twelve, but also "certain women, including Mary the mother of Jesus, as well as his brothers." (3) When Peter explained what was taking place, and did so by quoting the prophet Joel, he said that what was happening was the fulfillment of the prophecy, "your sons and your daughters shall prophesy." He could hardly use this argument if those "prophesying" were only twelve men.

(G) Discuss whether others received the Holy Spirit.

- Simply take for granted that after reading the material, the participants have come to the conclusion that more than the Twelve received the Spirit.
- Ask:
—Why do you think that in so many depictions of Pentecost it seems as if it was only the Twelve who received the Spirit? (Perhaps because such depictions come from a background in which it was taken for granted that only the Twelve, and certainly only men, could have such authority.)

(H) Remember that those present heard in their native tongues.

- Invite two students to roleplay a Jewish Christian and a Gentile Christian. Make certain that they understand these roles.
- Ask:
—What difference does it make to you, that those who heard did so in their own native tongues and not in the language of the original disciples? (This would be a blow to the ethnocentrism of the Jewish Christian and an affirmation of the Gentile, for it would show that from the beginning the Spirit was opening up doors for "different" people and for their differences.)
- Invite class members to imagine that they have just come to Jerusalem from Libya. People in Jerusalem do not seem to like you. Suddenly, you hear your language being spoken by a preacher. How do you think you might feel?

Optional Method

- Ask:
—Have you ever traveled in a foreign country and suddenly, in the least expected place, heard your language being spoken? How did you feel?

When we deal with the Holy Spirit, we are dealing with an awesome and somewhat unpredictable power. We must understand this as we proceed with this study.

(I) Consider the power of the Spirit.

- Remind students that the study book speaks of the surprising, terrifying power of the Spirit.
- Ask students to take their Bibles and open them just one page before the beginning of Acts.
- Give the following statement:

> Imagine that what you are holding is a bottle of nitroglycerin. It is a powerful substance. Properly used, it can open roads and help build cities. But it is also a very dangerous substance. Mishandle it, and it will blow you to pieces. Its power is available to you, but only if you take it very seriously and handle it with proper attention. In some ways, that is the way the Holy Spirit works. In this study, we shall be dealing with the Holy Spirit. But handle it carefully! Be prepared for it to change your whole life! Be prepared for it to challenge some of your most cherished assumptions! Now turn the page. Remember, you are holding a bottle of nitroglycerin! . . . From now on, and throughout this study, every time you read from the Book of Acts, every time you speak of the Spirit, handle with care! God may be speaking to you!

(J) Share expectations for your study.

- Ask what students expect of this study. Note expectations on newsprint or chalkboard.
- Enlarge your discussion to lead to greater expectations than mere information. Students will want to be informed. Yes. But above all we want to be transformed. We want to encounter that power that was made manifest in Pentecost. That is why we are here.

(K) Create a sense of expectation.

- Write the family names of four or five class participants (including yourself) in a column on the right of the chalkboard or newsprint. (If you do this before the class starts, and don't tell people why those names are up, you may create an interesting sense of expectation.)
- When you come to this point in the session, write in another column at the left edge of the chalkboard or newsprint the names of three or four of those who were present at Pentecost. (People such as Peter, James, John, and Mary.)
- Ask, while looking at the two columns:
—Were there any Browns, or Smiths, or Gonzálezes, or Yoons present at Pentecost? (Clearly not.)
—Did anybody among the early disciples speak English (or Spanish, or Korean, or whatever is the language of your class)? (Clearly not.)
—Thus, if the early church had continued moving only among the same people, and had continued speaking always the same language, would the gospel ever have reached us? (Probably not.)
- Conclude by saying: "No matter whether we know it or not, there is a long bridge—a bridge of many generations—spanning the distance between Pentecost and ourselves."
- At this point, ask participants if they wish to name any of the main sections of that bridge, that is, any part of the process that brought Christianity from then and them to here and us. Clearly, one important part of the process began on that Day of Pentecost.

(L) Study the map.

- Photocopy the map on the inside back cover naming the various places of origin of the people who witnessed the events of Pentecost. Share the map with students.
- Say:
"This map is the very first span on that long bridge of centuries. The very first step was that the gospel was spoken in the languages of all these people. Ever since, Christians have been translating the gospel, making it available to ever more people. At one point in that history, we were at the end of the bridge. The gospel was made available to us in our language and culture. Therefore, we must be willing to make the gospel available to other people in as many languages and cultures as possible—including those in our own nation."

Additional Bible Helps

The Jewish Festival of Pentecost
The Jewish Festival of Pentecost originally had to do with the bringing in of the harvest. Slowly, and especially after the Exile, when the people were no longer on the land, the meaning of the feast changed. As part of that change, one theme that was added to the significance of Pentecost was the giving of the law to Moses on Mt. Sinai. It is possible that the giving of the Spirit on the Day of Pentecost has significance for what Luke will be saying in the rest of the book. To those who objected to the admission of the Gentiles to the church on the basis of the law of Israel, Acts responded that the Spirit had shown that the way was open

to them. To those who would admit such Gentiles, but insisted that they must obey the law, and that male converts must be circumcised, Acts responded likewise that the Spirit had opened the way for the Gentiles to enter into the covenant without the law. The fact that the Spirit had come upon the church on the Day of Pentecost, the day of the giving of the law, can be seen as setting the foundation for this sort of argument.

The Feast of Pentecost was also significant in that there would be a great number of Jews from other parts of the world present in Jerusalem for that feast. Many of them would have come for the celebration of Passover, then remained the fifty days necessary to be there for Pentecost. The word that the NRSV translates as "living" in verse 5 does not necessarily mean that these Jews from all parts of the world were permanent residents of Jerusalem. That is why it has been suggested that the Feast of Pentecost was connected with the great variety of people present according to the account in Acts.

Consider the Physical Setting
One detail that may prove confusing to a careful reader of this story is the exact physical setting of the events told. At the beginning, we are told that "they were all together in one place," but we are not told what that place might be. Then in verse 2 we hear of "the house where they were sitting." This implied that they were indoors. [Although traditionally people have spoken of this event happening in the upper room where the Twelve lived (Acts 1:13) that would hardly be the place where the Christian community would meet.]

Yet after those who were gathered began to speak in various tongues, we are told that "the crowd gathered and was bewildered" (6), and the rest of the story implies that the disciples were some place where the crowds could both hear and watch them. Thus, there appears to be a shift of scene of which Luke does not apprise us.

This leaves us with two possible solutions. One is that there was a slight shift in scene from the beginning to the middle of the story. The narrative began indoors, inside the house where the disciples were sitting. Then, without our being told, it moved outside. In some ways, that is typical of the narrative in Acts, where many details are unrevealed, and the connections between various sections are not always clear.

The other possible solution is that "the house" is in fact the Temple. It was common for other authors, but not for Luke, to refer to the Temple as the "house." Still, some scholars suggest that in this particular case, this reference to "the house where they were sitting" may mean the Temple. Naturally, in that case there would have been others around, and the scene with the crowd could have taken place without a change of setting.

In verse 2, note the contrast between the word *suddenly* and the calm setting up until that moment (they were "sitting.") Again, since we already know the outcome of the story, we tend to think that they were gathered in great expectation, or that they were quite agitated. But that is not the picture given in Acts. They were calmly sitting together, apparently with no idea that something was about to happen, when these events took place.

Although the point was not made in the study book, you should note the words *like* in verse 2 and *as of* in verse 3. We usually think that there was a mighty wind and that tongues of fire descended on those who were gathered. But the words *like* and *as of* tell us that Luke was using images to try to describe something unique and indescribable. There was a sound. That sound was like that of a mighty wind. Something appeared among them. And it was best described as "divided tongues, as of fire."

Those who witnessed the event said that all who were speaking were "Galileans." While this is factually true, the exact meaning of the phrase in this context is not altogether clear. We know that very soon one of the pejorative titles given to Christians was "Galileans." We also know that Jews from Jerusalem tended to look down on Galileans as not quite as pure as themselves.

You may also be interested in the list of "nations" that appears in verses 9-11. Some of the names that appear there (Medes and Elamites) are strange in the sense that they were no longer used in the first century. They were ancient names of people mentioned in the Bible—and given precisely these names in the ancient Greek version of the Old Testament. Also, scholars point out that there are similar lists of "nations," and that Luke seems to have adapted one of these. That is why, if you simply look at a map of the region (except one expressly made to illustrate this list), you will not find all these names. Although they are all names of places, they were not all used at the same time.

In any case, do remember, that all these people were still Jews, or at least converts to Judaism (the "proselytes" of verse 10). The "Romans" are not Latin Romans, but Jews from Rome; and those from Egypt are not Egyptians, but Jews from that country. If you have any doubts on this point, look again at verse 5, which introduces all of these various people as "devout Jews from every nation under heaven."

That such Jews might speak different languages is not surprising. We have, for instance, the writings of a very well-educated Jew who lived in Alexandria roughly at this time, Philo. He writes in Greek, the language of the cultured and financial elite of Alexandria, and calls Greek "our language," while he refers to the tongue of his own Jewish people as "barbaric." Not only did he not know the Aramaic language that was spoken in Palestine, he was also ignorant of all but the bare rudiments of Hebrew.

2

Acts 4:1-22

AUTHORITY

LEARNING MENU

Again, keep in mind your class of learners and how they best learn. But surprise them a little too—and they may well surprise you! If you discover students are not reading the passage in their Bible and writing out answers to the Dimension 1 questions at home before class, suggest that they read the passage and answer the questions when they first come into the classroom. Other activities might be offered to arriving students who have already completed the questions.

Opening Prayer
> *God eternal,*
> *as you sent upon the disciples*
> *the promised gift of the Holy Spirit,*
> *look upon your church*
> *and open our hearts to the power of the Holy Spirit.*
> *Kindle in us the fire of your love*
> *and strengthen our lives for service in your kingdom;*
> *through your Son, Jesus Christ our Lord,*
> *who lives and reigns with you in the unity of the Holy*
> *   Spirit*
> *one God, now and forever. Amen.*

(From *Book of Common Worship.* ©1993 Westminster/John Knox Press)

Dimension 1: What Does the Bible Say?

(A) Answer study book questions.

- Briefly review answers to each of the Dimension 1 questions on page 12 of the study book.
- Rather than provide the correct answers, ask the class members what answers they found as they read the text.

(B) Review the text.

- Take a stack of 3-by-5 index cards and make sets of four cards each. One should read "SOLOMON'S POR-TICO," another "JAIL," and two "BEFORE THE COUNCIL." Preferably make a set for each expected participant in the class. (Or, if your class is very large, make several sets and then divide the class in groups.)
- As participants arrive, give one set of cards to each.
- Instruct students to put the cards in the order in which the action took place in the story. Cooperation with other students is encouraged!
- As the class begins, invite participants to share the order in which the cards were placed, giving the reasons for their particular ordering. (You may have one person

speak of the first card, another of the second, and so on.) In this manner you will review the text with them.

Optional Method

- If your class participants do not usually read the lesson material before your meeting, give students the cards as they arrive.
- Invite students to open their Bibles and read the text.
- As students read, ask them to attempt to put the cards in the order in which events occurred.

Teaching Tip

Take this opportunity to gently remind students that they will get much more out of the session when they read the lesson material before class.

Dimension 2: What Does the Bible Mean?

(C) Enjoy the story.

The passage we are studying is best understood in its entire context, which includes most of chapters 3–5. A helpful exercise for the entire class would be to see that these chapters are written in such a way that the story seems to repeat itself. This can best be seen by reading the two stories in parallel columns.

- Photocopy the chart below.
- Distribute the chart to each student.

Chapters	
3	**5**
3:1-10	5:12a
3:11	5:12b
3:12-26	
	5:13-16
4:1-3	5:17-18
4:4	
	5:19-21a
4:5-6	5:21b
	5:22-26
4:7	5:27-28
4:8-12	5:29-32
4:13-17	5:33-39
4:18	5:40
4:19-21a	5:41
4:21b-22	5:42
4:23-31	

- After distributing these parallel texts to the class, explain that the particular text we are studying is Acts 4:1-22, but that the chart is inclusive of two things:
—The background of the story in chapter 3, and
—A parallel story that is the continuation of the present one.
- Very quickly without reading word for word, retell the events in chapter 3, showing that the beginning of the entire episode was a miracle of healing and the preaching that ensued.
- Indicate that, although in much more general terms, that background is the same for the events told in chapter 5.
- Read the text listed in the left column, pausing to show any parallelisms with the text listed in the right.

Teaching Tip

If you used the cards with the names of places in Dimension 1, point out that the sequence is essentially the same, except that during the night the apostles were freed from prison, returning to preach at the Temple, presumably in Solomon's Portico. Distribute an additional card that says "SOLOMON'S POR-TICO" and ask participants to insert it in the appropriate place in their sets.

(D) Analyze power and prestige in the story.

- After the previous procedure, quickly divide the class in groups of two.
- Ask one partner in each pair to underline on the chart every word that indicates a person of power or prestige: elders, scribes, Sadducees, and other particular names of important people.
- Ask the other partner to do the same with terms that imply the more common or undistinguished people. These terms could be words such as *the people, uneducated,* or *ordinary.*
- As students finish this exercise, ask them what they did with the quote from Psalm 118: "This Jesus is
  'the stone that was rejected by you, the builders;
  it has become the cornerstone.' "
(Most likely, they did not mark anything. Yet, as you look at it, the point of the quote is precisely that there has been a reversal in matters of power and prestige.)
- Write the quote on newsprint or on a chalkboard.
- Analyze the quote, marking over it to emphasize your points. Circle the phrase "the stone that was rejected," and mark it with an arrow pointing down as you make the point that the theme is rejection—being rejected as utterly worthless and unusable. Circle the phrase "you, the builders," and mark it with an arrow pointing up. These were the leaders, the ones who were supposed to

know, whose judgment the people should have been able to trust. (Circle the phrase "has become the cornerstone" and mark it with a much larger arrow upward.) Things did not turn out as the builders expected. They rejected the one who was the center of the entire edifice.

● Ask:

—What does that tell us about the builders? (Circle them again, now with a big arrow downward.) They have been proven not to be such good builders after all! Thus, Peter was not just saying that he and John had the proper authority to preach and teach; he was also saying that these people who were judging him had lost that authority—and by implication also the authority to judge him.

(E) Explore the meaning of salvation.

● Instruct students to look closely at verses 9-12.
● Remind students that in Greek there is a single verb that we translate sometimes as "to heal" and sometimes as "to save," and a single noun that we translate sometimes as "salvation" and sometimes as "healing."
● Ask students to read verse 9, changing the word *healed* for *saved*.
● Read verse 12 as it now stands.
● Ask students to read verse 9 as it now stands and verse 12, substituting *healing* for *salvation*, and *healed* for *saved*.
● Insist that both readings are correct. Ask students to discuss the question:

—What does this imply for our understanding of both *salvation* and *healing*? (For *salvation*, it implies that it is much more holistic than we usually imagine. It includes not only the soul but the entire human being, and physical health is part of it. For *healing*, it implies that this is not just something that we owe to doctors or to medicines but something that ultimately must come from God and Christ, the same as salvation.)

(F) Look ahead at a future text.

● Although Acts 4:23-31 is not part of the text we are studying but its continuation, quickly look with the class at the passage and especially at verses 29-30. It is the response of the church to Paul and John's report on "what the chief priests and the elders had said to them" (23).
● Remind students of what caused the trouble to begin with: the healing of the lame man and the preaching that ensued.
● Remind students also that the Council had forbidden any further teaching or speaking in the name of Jesus.
● Note that in verses 29 and 30 the church prayed for two things, which were precisely the source of all their troubles: (1) "grant to your servants to speak your word

with all boldness"; and (2) "while you stretch out your hand to heal, and signs and wonders are performed through the name of your holy servant Jesus." In other words, the church prayed not for an end to its troubles, but precisely for more of the things that caused the trouble to begin with! (Since you will pick up on this point in Dimension 3, it should suffice for you to make the point at this time and move directly to Dimension 3.)

Dimension 3: What Does the Bible Mean to Us?

(G) Discuss.

If under Dimension 2 you have used more than one activity, and if your class period is limited to an hour, the lack of time may force you to present this third Dimension by means of a simple discussion.

● Ask:

—As you discover the conflict between the powerful and the early church in this story, does this make you think of situations today? (You may lead the discussion so that you focus first of all, as in the study book, on situations in other countries, particularly those where there are oppressive regimes. Next, you may wish to focus on our own situation. We have democratic institutions and freedoms; yet still quite often the powerful use their influence, not so much for the good of all, but to secure their power and continuing influence. Finally, move to the church itself and ask if there are groups in the church that react like the elders, scribes, and high priests of the biblical narrative, as if they had a monopoly on truth.)

● From this option, move to activity (I) or activity (J).

(H) Write a contemporary story.

For this option, you may need a bit more time. Therefore, it is feasible only if you arrive at this point and still have left about half of the class period.

● Having studied the text, divide the class into a number of teams or groups and give each the assignment of imagining a contemporary counterpart of the story we have studied. (In other words, they should change the characters, but the relationship should be similar.)
● Ask each of the groups to imagine and verbalize aloud the story in one of these contexts:

—The church trying to preach the gospel in a military dictatorship whose leaders fear that the church might be subversive;

—A local church trying to establish a halfway house for convicts and facing opposition from the community and the city council;

—A local church in which the young people want to start a mission in a disreputable neighborhood nearby, but some of the leadership oppose the project. (If the class is large enough to divide into more teams, assign the same theme to two or more groups.)

- Give each of these teams about ten to fifteen minutes to explore their story and to name someone to tell it to the rest of the class.
- Returning to the large-class format, give the representative from each group an opportunity to tell the story.
- After all groups have reported, allow for responses and commentaries on the part of the class.

(I) Construct a story.

This option is an intermediate between the simple discussion and the more elaborate construction of stories in activity (H).

- Suggest to the class that you will all together "write" (in reality, not commit to paper, but just make up as you go) a story that places the narrative we are studying in a more contemporary setting.
- On the chalkboard or newsprint, write a "cast of characters," listing the persons who appear in the biblical story: Peter, John, the man who was healed, the people, the priests, the Sadducees, the scribes, Annas, Caiaphas, and so forth.
- Paint the following picture:
  This is a fairly large and wealthy church in one of the "best" areas in town. In the church there is an old man named Peter, who sometimes has some fairly radical ideas. There is also a teenager, John, who is very active in the church, but who some say spends too much time with Peter. One day John and Peter meet a man with AIDS who is lonely and abandoned by all because of his disease. They decide to bring him to church with them.
- Invite students to pick up the story at this point. Let them name who will be the Sadducees, the priests, and so forth through the cast of characters listed. Let them imagine what the character's reactions and attitudes would be. Allow their imaginations to run as they "write" this imaginary story.
- At the end of the story, remind students of what the early church prayed for when it found itself in trouble (see Dimension 2); then close the session with prayer.

(J) Discuss how we handle difficult situations.

- Remind the class of what the early church did when they received the report of the Council's order to Peter and John.
- Ask:
—Is this what our church does when confronted with diffi-

cult situations?
- Give an example:
—In many churches, all controversial themes are forbidden. This avoidance includes matters on which we are fairly clear that the gospel directs us to take a certain stance, but society in general opposes it. A typical example in the 1950's was racial segregation. There were many churches who refused to take a stand on that issue, not because they did not know what the gospel demanded, but simply because they wished to avoid controversy at all cost.
- Ask:
—Is this what the early church did in our story?
—Can you think of any such issues today in our own community or nation? What might they be?
—In light of the prayer of the early church, what should we pray for in this regard?

(K) End the class session with a prayer.

God of all power and knowledge, the knowledge of your Word opens before us responsibilities and opportunities we had not even suspected. We know that on our own we do not have the power to do as you wish. Therefore we pray together that with the knowledge of your Word, you will give us the power to obey and follow it. We pray in the name of Jesus Christ, the only name in which there is hope and salvation, the rock that has been rejected by the master builders, but you have made the only sure foundation. Amen.

Additional Bible Helps

The People
The Greek word for people is *laós* from which our terms *lay* and *laity* are derived. It is a favorite word with Luke, who employed it twenty-nine times in his Gospel. Of those twenty-nine usages, only two have a parallel in the other Gospels. In other words, there are twenty-seven times in which the Gospel of Luke employs the term *laós* with no parallel in Matthew or Mark. This fact seems to imply that whatever independent source (or sources) Luke was using placed great stress on the *laós*. In Acts, *laós* is used even more frequently: a total of forty-eight times. In only two of these cases does the *laós* take a stance opposite to the early church.

The evolution of *laós* into *laity* is significant, for *laity* is normally used, not in reference to the entire church as the people of God, but in contrast with its ordained leadership. Note that in many passages (and certainly in the one we are studying), Luke and Acts uses *laós* in contrast with the religious and social leaders of Israel.

The Stone That the Builders Rejected

This quotation, taken from Psalm 118:22, appears to have been a favorite text of early Christians. In the Gospels it appears twice in the parallel passages regarding the parable of the wicked tenants in Matthew and Luke. In both cases, it is applied in such a way that the leaders of Israel realize that it was being used against them.

In Matthew Jesus quoted the psalm right after his parable of the wicked tenants (Matthew 21:42), and we are then told that "when the chief priests and the Pharisees heard his parables, they realized that he was speaking about them. They wanted to arrest him, but they feared the crowds, because they regarded him as a prophet" (21:45-46).

In Luke the context and the reaction are practically the same. Jesus quoted the psalm at the end of the parable (Luke 20:17) and the reaction of the powerful is the same: "When the scribes and chief priests realized that he had told this parable against them, they wanted to lay hands on him at that very hour, but they feared the people" (Luke 20:19).

Note in both cases the theme of the desire on the part of the elite to destroy Jesus, and their fear of the common people, who apparently would have reacted quite negatively to such an action. This theme is precisely what we saw running throughout the story in Acts that we are studying in this lesson.

The other place in the New Testament where Psalm 118:22 is quoted is 1 Peter 2:7. At the time of the writing of this epistle, the problem was no longer the leaders of Israel but disbelief in general. Therefore, there was no mention here of scribes or priests. But the theme of rejection and vindication continued. In this case, the epistle was addressed to people who were suffering rejection from society around them and, therefore, the passage from the Book of Psalms was used to remind them that Jesus too was rejected but has been made "the very head of the corner."

It is intriguing to note that in two of these passages, Acts and 1 Peter, the quotation was put on the lips (or the pen) of Peter. Apparently there was a fairly widespread tradition in the early church connecting Peter with this particular use of Scripture. Remember also that Peter was not his real name. His name was Simon, and it was Jesus who gave him the name Peter, which means "stone"!

In his *Commentary on Acts*, John Calvin also connected Peter's use of the passage from Psalm 118 with leaders of the church who use their power wrongly:
"Now we know Peter's object in quoting the Psalm; namely, lest the elders and priests should be so puffed up beyond reason on account of their honour that they should take to themselves authority and power to allow or disallow whatever they pleased. For it is evident that the stone that was rejected by the master builders is placed by the hand of God in the most important position to support the whole house.

"Furthermore, this happens not once only but is of necessity fulfilled every day; it ought at least to seem no strange or unlikely thing if today also the master builders reject Christ. . . . Let us briefly gather from this passage some things worth noting. As the leaders of the Church are called master builders, the name itself reminds them of their duty. Let them give themselves therefore wholly to the building of the temple of God. And since all men [sic] do not do their duty faithfully, let them observe what is the correct method of building aright, which is to keep Christ as the Foundation. Next, let them not mix straw or stubble in the building, but let them complete the whole building from pure doctrine. . . . Those who follow this example will have not Peter only, but also the Spirit of God as their guide" (*Calvin's Commentaries, The Acts of the Apostles 1-13*, edited by D.W. Torrance and T.F. Torrance, Wm. B. Eerdmans, 1965; pages 116-17).

3

**Acts
6:1-10**

CONFLICT

LEARNING MENU

Keep in mind the ways in which your class members learn best as well as their individual needs and interests, as you choose at least one learning activity from each of the three Dimensions that follow.

Opening Prayer

*Lover of concord,
you desire the unity of all Christians.
Set aflame the whole church with the fire of your Spirit.
Unite us to stand in the world as a sign of your love.
Amen.*

(From *Book of Common Worship.* ©1993 Westminster/John Knox Press)

Dimension 1:
What Does the Bible Say?

(A) Retell the story.

- By now most students should have discovered that they are expected to read their lesson material before the class session. Therefore, it may suffice simply to ask the class as a whole to retell the story of what they have read.

(B) Review study book questions.

- Form partners from among the members of the class.
- For a brief time, share individual reflections or answers to each of the questions on page 20 in the study book.
- At this point, discourage additional explanations or attempts to apply the text to life today.

(C) Get in touch with feelings.

- Keep the same partners as were used in activity (B) or, if you did not choose to use this activity, form partners for this activity.
- Provide each partnership with newsprint and markers.
- Identify personal reactions to conflict. Ask:
—Each of us has been involved in conflict at some time in our life. What were your reactions to it? Identify emotional reactions, physical reactions, and spiritual reactions.
—Is there anything common within our experience?

Dimension 2:
What Does the Bible Mean?

(D) Answer multiple choice questions.

- Print on newsprint the multiple choice questions listed below.
- Write only one question per sheet. Leave the first sheet blank so that the first question can only be read when you turn the cover page over.
- Begin to tell the biblical story. Remind the class that, according to what has already been said in Acts, when people brought money to be used for the needy, this money was given to the Twelve for them to manage (4:31). Therefore, any complaint or unhappiness ultimately implied a criticism of how the Twelve were managing the resources of the church.
- Invite students to imagine that they are the Twelve. Share the situation: The Twelve have spent all this time following Jesus. Some of them, such as Peter and John, have even been flogged for their faith. Now there are all these newcomers, and some of them have started to complain.
- Remove the cover sheet of the newsprint, revealing a sheet that reads, "Multiple Choice: Question One."
—If I had been one of the Twelve in that situation, I would have:
  (1) Ignored the complaints, hoping that no one would have the temerity to bring it out into the open.
  (2) Decided that the complainers were troublemakers who did not deserve to be heard.
  (3) Told the widows that they should be content with what they were getting, which after all was an act of charity.
  (4) Admitted that there was a problem and sought a solution.
- After a brief discussion in which you encourage people to be as frank as possible, remind them that what the Twelve did was answer number 4, from every human perspective a most unexpected thing.
- Remind students that Acts is essentially about how the Spirit works in the life of the church. In the decision that the Twelve made, there was a work of the Spirit just as surely as when they spoke in foreign tongues at Pentecost.
- Turn your attention to the congregation in Jerusalem. Share the following information:
Most likely the majority were still "Hebrews." Probably most of the property being sold had belonged to the Hebrews, especially if it was property located in Jerusalem or Judea. So, the numbers and the money were mostly on the Hebrew side; the Hellenists had begun to complain about the share they were getting.

- Turn over the sheet on the newsprint to reveal "Multiple Choice: Question Two."
—If I had been one of the Hebrews in that congregation, I would have:
  (1) Elected seven Hebrews to make sure that we kept the purse strings.
  (2) Elected a token Hellenist and six Hebrews.
  (3) Elected a proportional representation from both groups.
  (4) Set aside some money for the Hellenist widows and appointed a separate committee of Hellenists to manage that money.
  (5) Named seven Hellenists to manage all the money.
- After a brief discussion in which you encourage people to be as frank as possible, remind them that what the congregation did was number 5, from every human perspective a most unexpected thing.
- Once again, point out that Acts is about the work of the Spirit, and that here again we see the Spirit at work in a decision that the church made.
- Turn your attention to Stephen. Share the following: Stephen was a Hellenist and as such he was not well regarded by most people in Jerusalem. For the first time in Acts the opponents of Christianity managed to recruit the support of both the elite and the common people among the Jews. Stephen probably knew that. He had been named to help manage and distribute the resources of the church among the needy. That, in itself, was an important job. He had no need to go out to the rest of the community and get himself in trouble proclaiming the name of Jesus or arguing with anyone.
- Turn another sheet on the newsprint pad, to reveal: "Multiple Choice: Question Three."
—If I had been Stephen in that situation, I would have:
  (1) Kept myself so busy with my job that I would have had no time to go and argue with anyone.
  (2) Told myself that my job was to see to the distribution, then stay out of trouble.
  (3) Upon meeting someone who had not heard the gospel, sent one of the Twelve to them (after all, that was their job).
  (4) Continued speaking and testifying, even though my situation got worse and worse.
- After a brief discussion in which you encourage people to be as frank as possible, remind them that what Stephen did was number 4, from every human perspective a most unexpected thing.
- Once again, point out that Acts is about the work of the Spirit. We see in Acts the Spirit at work in a decision that a believer made.
- End this option with a general discussion of how we see the Spirit at work in no less dramatic a fashion than at Pentecost or in the miracle of healing the lame man at the Temple gate.

Optional Method

- Simply have a discussion in which you explore the unexpected elements in the text.
- Tell the class to read the story as if they had never heard it before and imagine that it refers, not to the church, but to a business in our community today.
- At each turn in the story, help the class to see the unexpected decision that was made. (Use the questions in the above activity for hints as to what these decisions might be.) As in activity (D), point out that where the Spirit was not explicitly mentioned, Luke was still trying to show the manner in which the Spirit worked in the church.

(E) Share information from Additional Bible Helps.

- In this option, you are going beyond what was said in the study book. Read the information provided under Additional Bible Helps, page 17.
- Explain to students that all the people mentioned in verse 9 were Hellenistic Jews.
- Show on a map each of the places named, so that the class may see that some of them were quite far from Jerusalem. If you have access to the *Bible Teacher Kit*, (Abingdon, 1994), use the wall map entitled, "New Testament Palestine." If you do not have this map, use a wall-sized map of first century Palestine or refer students to the maps in the back portions of the study book.
- It is interesting to note that Stephen, himself a Hellenist, found that his most persistent enemies were other Hellenists. One would imagine that the fact that there were now Hellenists among the Christian leadership would in fact make Christianity more attractive to other Hellenists. Eventually that became the case. But in the story of Stephen, his worst enemies were other Hellenists.
- Lead students to discuss why Stephen's worst enemies were other Hellenists. (Obviously, all that we really know is what the text tells us. But it is easy to imagine that Hellenistic Jews, already regarded askance by the more local Hebrew Jews, would have looked upon Stephen as a further threat to their own standing. The more Hellenistic Jews turned to Christianity, the more the Hebrew Jews would look upon all Hellenists with suspicion.)
- Note also that the result was that, for the first time in the Book of Acts, "the people" took the side of "the elders and the scribes" (see Acts 6:12). In other words, the elite and the general population were on the same side, against Stephen the Christian.
- Ask:
—What do you think would have been the reaction of the elite that for so long had been trying to put pressure on

Christians, but had refrained from doing so "for fear of the people"? (In this discussion, remember that, although it was the Hellenists who stirred things up, it was the Council that condemned Stephen.)

Dimension 3: What Does the Bible Mean to Us?

(F) Engage your imagination.

- Invite participants (no matter what their primary ethnic backgrounds may be) to imagine that they are part of a mostly white, English-speaking congregation sharing a building with an ethnic minority congregation. (You may decide what particular ethnic minority this would be.)
- Describe the situation:
—The physical facilities are rather large, built at a time when the white congregation was growing and prosperous. There is an endowment that takes care of most maintenance expenses.
—Your own white congregation is not as large as it used to be, for the demographics of the area have changed. It is still an active congregation, where you and many others find a true spiritual home.
—The ethnic minority congregation is growing rapidly. Although it is still not quite as large as yours, it seems evident that it will soon be. It is also younger, and its adults all attend Sunday school, with the result that their Sunday school is much larger than yours. Since you were here first, your Sunday school still uses the best facilities, and the ethnic minority Sunday school, which meets at the same time, uses an old gym where they are overcrowded, with several classes meeting in various corners of the old basketball court.
—You have heard that there is some unhappiness among the members of the ethnic minority congregation. They know that your educational building is being used at half of its capacity, and they would like to move some of their classes into classrooms that are not being used. They do not know how such a request will be received, and therefore, instead of presenting that request, they are simply talking and grumbling about the situation.
- Ask:
—What would you do? (Here are some options, but there may be others:)
  (1) I would inform the white pastor and council on ministries, asking them to take the initiative in talking with the ethnic minority leaders.
  (2) I would tell the ethnic minority leaders that they should stop the grumbling by presenting a formal petition to the appropriate authorities in the white congregation.

(3) I would tell the ethnic minority leaders that they should remember that they are our guests and should stop all the ungrateful grumbling among their people.

(4) I don't want to be labeled as a gossip; therefore I would just ignore the grumbling, hoping that it will go away.

● Now ask the class (again, no matter what its own real ethnic background may be) to reverse the situation and imagine that the class is part of the ethnic minority congregation.

—Say: "You have heard the grumbling. What will you do?" (Again, here are some options:)

(1) I would just ignore it. Eventually it will either go away or get so bad that something will have to be done.

(2) I would add my voice to the grumblers with the hope that eventually something will have to be done.

(3) I would tell those who are grumbling that they should be grateful for the hospitality of the white congregation and quit grumbling.

(4) I would tell the leaders of my own congregation so that they may deal with the grumblers.

(5) I would encourage the leaders of my congregation to speak to the white leaders.

Optional Method

● This option is really a continuation of activity (F).
● Describe the change in scene:
—Imagine that a petition has gone from the ethnic minority congregation to the white congregation. Ask the study group to roleplay a meeting of the committee in charge of responding to that petition.
● Invite participants to discuss the petition. (In order to make the discussion more lively and to encourage people to raise objections they would otherwise not dare voice, invite half of the class to argue in favor of the petition and half to argue against it.)
● After a few minutes of this discussion, read again Acts 6:1-6.
● Ask:
—Do you see any connection between this Scripture and the situation we have discussed?

(G) Consider other divisions.

● Follow a similar procedure used in activity (F).
● Consider divisions other than race:
—You are a church in a rural area that is becoming part of suburbia. The church has an excellent program dealing with various rural concerns. The changing situation brings tensions within the congregation itself.
—You are a church in a working-class neighborhood into which professionals are now moving.
—You are an ethnic minority church in an area into which another ethnic minority is moving.
—You are a part of a discussion at the district or conference level about devoting church development funds to start a new congregation in an area where people are very poor, therefore there is little chance that the new church will become self-supporting in the near future.

(H) Look for modern parallels to Stephen's situation.

● This activity builds on an earlier activity (E). Having discussed how it was that Stephen's worst enemies were other Hellenists like himself, and that in that opposition they made common cause with the Council, suggest that there are parallel situations today.
● On this point, you may offer an example:
It has been noted that in many cases, when a woman becomes pastor of a church, and there is opposition to having a woman pastor, some of the most belligerent in that opposition are other women in the congregation. One would expect that all women would be in favor of having a woman pastor. Such is not the case.
● Consider the situation in the time of Stephen. On newsprint or chalkboard, list the "players" who were a part of that situation.
● Record your list in two columns, similar to that offered below:
—The Jewish Hellenists. They are looked at askance, and must protect their prestige. That is why they try to disassociate themselves from Stephen.
—Stephen, who threatens that prestige by becoming a Christian leader.
—The Council, which is not particularly in favor of the Hellenists, nevertheless welcomes their support to get at Stephen and the Christians.
● Invite the class to name the "players" in the modern example provided. List them across from their corresponding "players" in the biblical story. Use the chart below to "prime the pump."

Stephen	Woman pastor
Hellenistic Jews	Other women
Council	Men who fear losing their power

● Finally, give students an opportunity to discuss any further insights they may have gained from this comparison.

(I) Close the session.

● Close your session in song. Choose hymns from your congregational hymnbook that speak of reconciliation. Two possibilities include the following:
—"Blest Be the Tie That Binds" (No. 557 in *The United Methodist Hymnal*)

—"Help Us Accept Each Other" (No. 560 in *The United Methodist Hymnal*)

Additional Bible Helps

The Election of the Deacons

In many older Bibles, the passage we are studying is called "The Election of the Seven Deacons." The title in the NRSV is different, and that in the entire lesson we have refrained from using the title "deacon" (even though traditionally people speak of Stephen and Philip as "deacons").

The reason why these people have been called "deacons" is that in verse 2 where the Twelve speak of "waiting" on tables, the verb *diakonein* has the same root as "deacon." Out of this usage the tradition developed that these seven were the first deacons of the church.

The problem is that later (in verse 4) the Twelve reserved for themselves the *service* of the word, and the term used, *diakonía*, has the same root. Thus, if we are to call the seven "deacons" for that reason, the Twelve should also be given the same title.

We know that from a very early date there were "deacons" (both men and women) in the Christian church (see, for instance, Romans 16:1). We do not know for certain that these seven had that title. As a matter of fact later on in Acts (11:30), we shall encounter the "elders" (presbyters) of the church in Jerusalem. Since these are clearly not the Twelve, some scholars suggest that they may be these seven (or their successors, for at that time Stephen was dead and at least Philip had left Jerusalem). Also the only place in Acts where one of the seven is given a title is Acts 21:8, where Philip is called "the evangelist."

"Wait on Tables"

The phrase "wait on tables" has an ambiguity in Greek that is impossible to translate into English. That is why you will note that the NRSV has a note suggesting that it could also be translated as "keep accounts."

At that time, a "table" could mean both the place where one ate and the place where one counted money—and, by extension, the bank. In Luke 19:23, where the NRSV translates, "put my money into the bank," the Greek actually says "the table." In consequence, the phrase in Acts 6:2, which the NRSV translates as "to wait on tables," could mean what we actually understand by that phrase; it could also mean to manage funds and keep accounts; or it could even mean "to do the banking." Therefore, the exact duties of these seven are difficult to determine.

In modern Western languages, there is a similar connection, not with the word *table*, but with the word *bench*. Thus, several of these languages use the same or similar words for both: German: *bank*; Spanish and Portuguese: *banco*; Danish: *banke/bænk*. When you think about it, you can see that even in English there still is

some resemblance between the words *bench* and *bank*.

A Problem of Interpretation

Verse 9 presents some problems of interpretation and translation. In the Greek, the number of synagogues to which the verse alluded is not clear. From the translation in the NRSV, it appears that there was one synagogue called "of the Freedmen," and that in that synagogue there were Cyrenians, Alexandrians, Cilicians, and people from the Roman province of Asia. In fact the text may refer to two different synagogues, and even to five.

To complicate matters, the very phrase *of the Freedmen* is odd, for all the other names refer to a place of origin; this one refers to a social status. It has been suggested that in fact they were Jews from Rome, who had been taken there when the Romans conquered Judea, and had later been freed. Hence the name "of the Freedmen." (The ancient Armenian version, instead of "the Freedmen," says "the Libyans." Some scholars think that this was the original text, which some early scribe miscopied.)

In any case, what is important is that all of these people apparently came from regions outside of Judea and west of Jerusalem, and that they therefore would be classified as "Hellenists."

Four of those points of origin are clear, and one is doubtful (look them up on the map): (1) Cyrene; (2) Alexandria; (3) Cilicia; (4) Asia (then the name given to the province around Ephesus); (5) perhaps Rome or Libya.

The Subject of the Book

The study book indicates that this passage is an important transition point. From this point on the Twelve play a lesser role. (Peter and the church in Jerusalem were again the center of attention in chapters 10-12, but after this time they appeared with less and less frequency.) Thus, although the traditional name of the book is "Acts of the Apostles," the apostles are not in fact the subject of the book.

Nor were the seven the subject. The rest of chapter 6 and all of 7 deal with Stephen; chapter 8 deals with Philip and his ministry. The other five are not mentioned again and Philip only briefly in 21:8.

You could say that Paul is the main character of the book, for he appeared briefly in chapter 9, and from chapter 13 on he was the dominant figure. But even that is not a satisfactory answer, for if the book was mainly about Paul and his ministry it would not end abruptly without telling us whatever became of Paul.

In fact, the book is really about the Holy Spirit! All characters come in and then disappear, in order to show what the Spirit is doing. No one, not even the Twelve or Paul, is followed throughout the book, because ultimately its subject is not a person or a group of persons but the Holy Spirit acting in the early church.

Acts 8:4-25

LEARNING MENU

Keep in mind the ways in which your class members learn best as you choose at least one learning activity from each of the three Dimensions that follow. Remember that Dimension 1 activities explore what the Bible says and put biblical events into a larger geographical and historical context. Dimension 2 activities explore what Jesus meant according to the writer of the Acts of the Apostles and how Luke's original readers and hearers heard it. Dimension 3 activities explore what the passages mean in students' personal lives, congregational lives, and lives as disciples in God's world.

Opening Prayer
God of all might and power,
we praise you that
you forged your church in the fire of the Spirit,
and breathed life into your people
that we might be the body of Christ. . . .
By your Spirit,
baptize us again with your flame of faith,
fill us with the breath of zeal,
inspire us with the witness of martyrs and saints,
and send us forth into your world
to live Christ's life in power and compassion.
Amen.

(From *Book of Common Worship.* ©1993 Westminster/John Knox Press)

Dimension 1: What Does the Bible Say?

(A) Engage in map study.

- Provide a wall map of Palestine in the first century. (Leaders having access to *Bible Teacher Kit*, Abingdon, 1994, will find the map "Palestine in New Testament Times" helpful.)
- Ask class members to name where the story took place. (Read the article in the Additional Bible Helps section at the end of this chapter, "Did Events Take Place in Samaria?" The question of the exact city is discussed. You can at least point to the region of Samaria.)
- Name the main characters.
- Invite class members to review the geographic movement of the main characters, as far as can be told from the text. (Philip began in Jerusalem and went to Samaria. Simon Magus was in Samaria all the time. Peter and John came from Jerusalem at a later date. They then returned to Jerusalem, preaching in the villages of Samaria. Philip was still in Samaria at the end of the story.)

(B) Tell the story of Philip's ministry in Samaria.

- Ask a class member to tell the story of Philip's ministry in Samaria, drawing upon information in the Scripture passage and the study book.
- Allow other members to add details or to correct details. Your goal at this point is not to get into the interpretation of the text, but simply to have the class review what the text actually says.

Dimension 2: What Does the Bible Mean?

(C) Focus on Simon Magus.

An interesting way to help the class focus on the text is to focus on Simon Magus.

- Invite a class member in advance to research as much information as possible regarding this character. As a starting place, the researcher can read what is said about Simon Magus in the Additional Bible Helps section on page 22 of this guide.
- The researcher should take no more than five minutes to focus on the various traditions and legends that have developed around Simon Magus.
- Ask students if the traditions and legends seem to be based on what Acts tells us about Simon Magus or based on fantasy or imagination.

Teaching Tip

Use this opportunity both to have the class focus on the text of Scripture and to raise awareness of how easy it is to read into a text things that are not there. Make certain that the researcher making the presentation understands beforehand that this is what you are doing. Otherwise, this person might think that you have simply asked him or her to do all this work, just to tell the class that it is all wrong. Or, if you prefer, you may have the same person tell about the legends and then add how wrong they are.

(D) See a movie.

- Visit your local video rental shop.
- Secure a videotape of the movie, *The Silver Chalice* (made by Warner Bros. in 1954 and directed by Victor Saville).
- Select the very short scene where Simon Magus appears and show it to the class.
- Ask: Is the Simon you see in the movie at all like the Simon Magus you had imagined when reading the text from Acts?

- Allow for some discussion, helping the class to review the story as Acts tells it.

(E) List the main characters in the story.

- Before class, write on chalkboard or newsprint the main characters in the story, as follows: Philip, the people in the city, Simon Magus, Simon Peter, and John.
- Give chalk or a marker to one of the class participants.
- Tell students that you are going to read the story, stopping at several points, and will ask whether a particular person or group appears to be powerful or not.
- When students indicate that a character was powerful, have the person with the chalk or marker put an arrow pointing upwards next to that person's name; when powerless, the arrow should point downward.
- Read 8:4-5a (stopping at the word *Samaria*).
- Ask: Does Philip appear powerful here, or not? (Note that he was fleeing from persecution.)
- After a brief discussion, the person can indicate on the chalkboard or newsprint the appropriate arrow.
- Read 8:5-7.
- Ask: Does Philip appear powerful here?
- After a brief discussion, the person can indicate on the chalkboard or newsprint the appropriate arrow.
- Ask: What about the people of the city?
- After discussion, add the corresponding arrow.
- Read 8:8.
- Ask: What about the people of the city now? (Again, follow the same procedure.)
- Read 8:9-11.
- Ask the question about Simon and follow the same procedure.
- Ask: When the people of the city were following Simon, which direction would the arrow point?
- After discussion, have the arrow drawn.
- Read 8:12-13.
- Ask: What about the people now?
—What about Simon?
- Draw the appropriate arrows.
- Skip to 8:17 and read it. Ask:
—What about the people in the city now? Draw the arrow.
—What about Peter? Again, add an arrow.
—What about Peter when he was a fisherman in Galilee? How would you have drawn the arrow then?
- Read 8:18-23. Ask the same questions about Peter and Simon Magus and have the appropriate arrows drawn.
- Read 8:24. (You may wish to have a fuller discussion on this point. Simon admitted his error and asked for prayers on his behalf.)
- Ask:
—Does this admission merit an arrow pointing up or one pointing down?

—In other words, when you admit your error and ask for help, does that give you power, or take it away? (Obviously, it depends on how you understand power.)

Teaching Tip

Since they are not crucial for the rest of the session, you may wish to avoid the various problems related to the interpretation of verses 15 and 16. If the class raises them, however, you should deal with them as briefly and as clearly as possible. You can probably best accomplish this by means of a brief presentation on the basis of the material under Additional Bible Helps, page 22, of this guide. Study that material and prepare for that possibility.

Dimension 3:
What Does the Bible Mean to Us?

(F) Teach through a mini-lecture.

A Contrast Between Two Simons

Peter had been a fisherman. Although apparently he and some partners owned their fishing boat, that certainly did not make him a particularly important or powerful person. He had then gone to Jerusalem, where as a Galilean he would not have been particularly welcome or appreciated. At a point, he had fled from those who accused him of having been one of Jesus' followers.

He was among those who received the power of the Spirit at Pentecost. The Spirit had made him a bold and powerful witness to Jesus. We have already seen that, when he appeared before the Council, his boldness amazed them—particularly since he was obviously "uneducated and ordinary" (Acts 4:13). The powerless fisherman from Galilee had received a power that the powerful in the Council could not understand.

Then there was Simon Magus. If anything is clear about him in Acts' depiction of his life before Philip went to Samaria, it is that he was a powerful and prestigious person. (You may read again verses 10-11 to see just how powerful he was.)

When Philip came to the city and amazed the entire population, including Simon himself, that was something Simon could understand. Therefore, he believed, was baptized, and began following Philip wherever he went.

When Peter and John came to the city and Simon Magus saw that the power of the Holy Spirit could apparently be given by the imposition of hands, he

tried to buy that power. His mistake was that he did not realize that this power was entirely different from that which he had enjoyed and understood as a magician and a man of prestige. This was not a power that could be bought or earned.

In a nutshell, what we have here is the contrast between Simon Peter, a powerless man who had been empowered by the Spirit, and Simon Magus, a powerful man who thought he could transfer his power in the city into power in the Spirit.

This point is important because we must learn to distinguish between the power that society gives (or that one takes from society) and the power of the Spirit. The two are not interchangeable. To confuse them damages the church.

(G) Think about power today.

- Ask students to make a list of the most popular, powerful, and prestigious people in your community and/or in our nation.
- On chalkboard or newsprint, list sport stars, entertainers, financiers, and so forth. (Choose three or four of these people. Make them as different from each other as possible.)
- Divide the class into three or four groups, assign one of those famous people to each group, and invite them to imagine that this particular person has moved into the neighborhood and begun attending our church.
- Ask:
—How would you react?
—Do you think you would deal with that person as you would with any other sinner needing repentance and hope?
—Would you give that person special privileges?
—Would you worry that without such privileges and special treatment that person would leave?
- Allow the groups to discuss these questions for a few minutes. Then bring them back together for reports and a general discussion on how this activity relates to the story of Simon Magus and Simon Peter.

(H) Tape religious programmings.

- During the week, tape some of the popular religious TV programs during which famous people give their witness. Look particularly for testimonies of sport and entertainment figures.
- Select three or four minutes of tape that show how these people are received and treated.
- Show this tape to the class and ask:
—Are these people receiving special treatment because society at large grants them special honors?

—If so, is there the danger that, like Simon Magus, they may be trading their prestige in society for prestige and power in the Christian community?

—If so, what do you think Peter would have said?

(I) Imagine your church is impoverished.

• Ask the class to imagine that your church is a fairly poor church. Share the following information:

> You can hardly meet your budget every month, and you are having difficulty meeting payments on the mortgage of $100,000 on your building. The main source of employment in your town is a small factory, built and still owned by a family after whom the town itself is named.
>
> A few months ago the owner of the factory, who had not seemed a particularly religious man, surprised all of you by beginning to attend your church. He attended regularly and eventually asked to be baptized and to join the church. There is no doubt that he is sincere, that there has been a change in his life.
>
> Now he has made the church a strange offer. He is willing to pay off the entire mortgage. But he will do that only if he is made a member of the finance committee and of the pastor/parish relations committee.

• Invite four to six students to sit in the middle of the class (or in front of it) and to pretend that they are a committee discussing this offer.

• Ask them to consider the following questions:

—Will they accept the offer or not?

—In either case, how will they respond to him?

—What will they tell the congregation?

—What will they tell reporters from the local newspaper who may want to report this news?

• Participants do not have to come to a decision. Simply give them a few minutes to discuss the issues involved; then turn to the class at large for a general discussion of this question: What would Peter have said in such a situation?

(J) Discuss names of churches.

• Share the following informtion:

—For a long time it has been customary to name churches after significant biblical figures: The Cathedral of St. Paul, St. James United Methodist Church, St. Luke the Evangelist Episcopal Church, and so forth.

—Churches have also been named after important points of Christian doctrine: Church of the Holy Trinity, Chapel of the Resurrection, Church of the Transfiguration, Church of the Annunciation, and so forth.

—Others are named after founders of various Christian traditions: John Wesley United Methodist Church, John Calvin Presbyterian Church, Susannah Wesley United Methodist Church, and so forth.

—Many have traditionally been named after people who gave to the poor all they had: St. Francis Roman Catholic Church, The Church of St. Basil, and The Church of St. Ambrose.

—In more recent decades, however, a different type of name has become quite common. These are the names of people who have financially backed the church: John and Mary Smith United Methodist Church, Betty Brown Memorial Church, and so forth.

• Ask and discuss these questions:

—Do you see any significance in this change in the way names are chosen for churches?

—Does it make any difference whether one names a church for someone who, like St. Francis, became poor for the sake of the gospel or for someone who simply was able to write a large check?

(K) Explain the term *simony*.

• Explain:

In the Middle Ages one of the signs of corruption in the church was the practice of buying and selling ecclesiastical positions. A man would buy a bishopric as an investment, hoping to make a profit from the tithes and offerings as well as from selling parishes to prospective priests. As the practice grew, there were many who opposed it, and gave it the name of "simony" after Simon Magus, who tried to buy the power of the Holy Spirit with money.

• Ask:

—What do you think of the practice of buying and selling positions in the church?

—Would it be an appropriate fund-raising strategy? Why or why not?

—Do you think that those who opposed it were right in calling it "simony"? Why or why not?

—Do you think it is true that right now in the United States, there are denominations where salary considerations are fundamental in the process of matching churches and pastors?

—Do you know of cases where a large and wealthy church pays a higher salary than a poorer church, and thus has their "pick" of the pastors, while the poorer church must take whomever it can afford? (This situation certainly can happen in denominations where congregations call their pastors, and pastors decide whether or not to accept such a call based on the salary offered.)

—Is it also true in any way of denominations where pastors are appointed by a bishop or a cabinet?

—How is this situation different from medieval simony? How is it similar?

—How is it better or worse?

—Having read the story of Peter and Simon Magus, what do you think Peter would have said about these situations?

Additional Bible Helps

Hebrews Versus Hellenists

In verse 4 Luke indicated that Christians were scattered as a result of persecution. In verse 14 Luke indicated that the apostles were still in Jerusalem. The explanation for this development probably lies in the distinction between "Hebrews" and "Hellenists," which we studied in last week's lesson. Apparently the worst of the persecution, for the time being, was against the Hellenists who had become Christians. Thus, people such as Philip were forced to flee, while the apostles, who were Hebrews, were able to stay. You may also be interested to know that the story of the church in Antioch, which we shall be studying in two weeks, also begins with the phrase "those who were scattered" (Acts 11:19).

Did Events Take Place in Samaria?

Acts 8:5 tells us that these events happened in "the city of Samaria." Other manuscripts say "a city of Samaria." No matter which of the two is the original, it does not necessarily mean that the events took place in the city whose name was Samaria. In the first century, there was no city by that name. "Samaria" was the name of the capital of the Northern Kingdom, Israel. Herod had rebuilt it and given it the name of "Sebaste," which was the Greek equivalent of "Augusta," in honor of Augustus Caesar. Therefore, although it was in Samaria, it was mostly a Gentile city. For that reason, many commentators think that "the city of Samaria" to which Acts refers is Shechem, at that time the most important city for the Samaritans. There is also a very ancient tradition connecting Simon Magus with Shechem.

Philip Proclaimed the Messiah

Acts 8:5 tells us that Philip proclaimed "the Messiah" to them. Apparently there was among the Samaritans a very high level of expectation of the Messiah—whom they called *Taeb* or the Restorer. It has been pointed out that the miracles attributed to Philip in Acts 8:7 were mostly acts of restoration and, therefore, could be seen as signs that the *Taeb* had indeed come.

More Difficult Questions

Verses 15 and 16 pose several difficult questions to which unfortunately there is no agreed upon answer. One such question is what is meant by saying that "they had only been baptized in the name of the Lord Jesus." This text has been used in support of those who claim that early Christian baptism was only in the name of Jesus, and who therefore reject the more common trinitarian formula. Others counter that argument by pointing out that according to this text such baptism is clearly deficient.

Then there is the question of the relationship between baptism and receiving the Holy Spirit. Some claim that this text proves that, after water baptism, there must be a second baptism by the Holy Spirit. Others respond that, on the contrary, this text shows that it was a defective baptism that required the later baptism of the Spirit.

Finally, there is the question of the authority and function of the apostles, for on the basis of this text, some have claimed that, while any Christian can baptize, only the apostles or their successors, the bishops, can lay their hands on a believer for the reception of the Holy Spirit—that is to say, for confirmation. Thus, these two verses, whose meaning simply cannot be completely determined, have been used as support for very different positions, from the most extreme anti-trinitarian and charismatic to the most traditional, hierarchical and catholic.

Simon Magus

Simon Magus is well known to most of us, in part because he has become a sort of theological scapegoat on whom tradition has put the blame for all sorts of evil. In the ancient church and in many history books to this day, he is credited with being the creator of Christian gnosticism—probably the worst doctrinal threat to the church in the second century. Sometime in the third or fourth century, an unknown writer (or writers) made him the villain of a series of episodes in which Simon Peter and Simon Magus matched their miracle-making might (in documents usually called the *Recognitions of Clement* and the *Clementine Homilies*). In the Middle Ages those who sought to reform the church gave the name of "simony" to the practice of buying and selling ecclesiastical offices. In more recent times, Hollywood has produced a movie on early Christianity in which Simon Magus was again the arch-villain who sought to imitate and to outdo Peter's miracles.

On Simon and gnosticism, see *A History of Christian Thought*, vol. 1, revised edition, by Justo L. González (Abingdon, 1987; pages 131-32).

On the later legend about Simon, see the *Recognitions of Clement* and the *Clementine Homilies* in *The Ante-Nicene Fathers*, vol. VIII (Wm. B. Eerdmans, reprint of an 1886 edition; pages 77-346).

On simony in the Middle Ages, see any general church history book. For instance, *A History of the Christian Church*, revised edition, by Williston Walker (Scribner's, 1959; pages 200, 205). See also *The Story of Christianity*, vol. 1, by Justo L. González (Harper Collins, 1984; pages 280, 283-86).

Finally for later fiction about Simon Magus, you may wish to see the movie, *The Silver Chalice*, mentioned in activity (D) or refer to the novel by Thomas B. Costain on which it is based.

5

Acts 9:1-30

CONVERSION

Opening Prayer
Almighty God,
at the feast of Pentecost
you sent your Holy Spirit to the disciples,
filling them with joy and boldness
to preach the gospel;
empower us with that same Spirit
to witness to your redeeming love
and draw all people to you;
through Jesus Christ our Lord,
who lives and reigns with you and the Holy Spirit,
one God, now and forever. Amen.

(From *Book of Common Worship.* ©1993 Westminster/John Knox Press)

Dimension 1:
What Does the Bible Say?

(A) Answer study book questions.

As an introduction to the entire lesson, the first question under Dimension 1 (study book, page 37) could be quite useful.

- Ask students to share with the class how they have answered that question. (Actually, there are only three earlier references to Saul in Acts.)
- He was first introduced in Acts 7:58 at the moment of the stoning of Stephen, where we are told that "the witnesses laid their coats at the feet of a young man named Saul."
- Later, at the end of that story in 8:1, we learn that "Saul approved of their killing him."
- It is in the very next passage telling of the persecution against the church in Jerusalem that we learn that Saul was a leading figure in that persecution: "But Saul was ravaging the church by entering house after house; dragging off both men and women, he committed them to prison." Thus, all that we know of Saul before we come to the moment of his conversion appears between 7:58 and 8:3.

- Record student answers on the chalkboard or newsprint, as background for the story we are about to study.

(B) Discuss your knowledge of Paul.

- Ask:
—What do we know about Paul before his conversion? (In other words, although this is all that Acts tells us before this point, later, both in the same Book of Acts and in Paul's Epistles, we will learn more about him.)
- Write a brief summary of student answers on the chalkboard or newsprint. (We know, for instance, that Paul was from Tarsus, that he was a Pharisee, that he was a Roman citizen, that he studied under Gamaliel.)
- If you have access to *Bible Teacher Kit* (Abingdon, 1994), share information from the article "The World of Paul" by Justo L. González and Catherine G. González, pages 63-66.

(C) Consider three main characters.

- Invite students to take a moment and think about three of the main characters in this story: Saul, Ananias, and Barnabas.
- Think in particular about which of the three characters they would rather have as a friend and why.
- After allowing a couple of minutes for thinking about that question, ask people to share their responses; discuss them.

Teaching Tip

Your purpose is to encourage the class to look at biblical personages not as flat, cardboard-like figures, but as real persons whom students might meet on the street or at church, persons with whom they would interact.

Dimension 2:
What Does the Bible Mean?

The story is well known. You will need to use some innovative method to make it come alive in a new way. The following are some options for doing that:

(D) Imagine yourself as Ananias.

- Provide paper and pencil to each participant.
- Invite each student to imagine that they are Ananias. Say:
"You joined the church about two years ago. It was a marvelous fellowship of love and praise. Although some of your neighbors ridiculed you, the experience of being part of this community was well worth it. Then

persecution broke out. You had to flee Jerusalem, leaving behind the business that had sustained your family for generations, making and selling pottery. Now you are in Damascus, relieved that there is no persecution here. Still, you miss your home and shop, where you and your family would still be were it not for the persecution.
"Now you hear that Saul, the terrible leader of the persecution in Jerusalem, has obtained letters from the high priest and is coming to Damascus to extend the persecution here." (brief silence)
—How do you react to that bit of news?
—What do you think?
- Instruct class members to write down their reactions.
- Allow one minute for students to record reactions.
- Say:
"It's been a few weeks since you first heard of Saul's plans, and you know that he is now well on his way to Damascus. Although by now you have set up a small shop in Damascus and invested in it all your meager resources, you are considering the possibility of packing up and leaving once more. Perhaps you will have to move to Antioch, or even farther away to Athens or to Rome. You ask, 'Why won't this Saul leave the church alone?' Someone comes and gives you strange news indeed. They have just seen Saul arrive at Damascus. Apparently he had some sort of accident along the road for he was blind, appeared shaken, and had to be led by the hand."
- Ask students to imagine what their reaction would be if they were Ananias.
- Once again, provide students with time to record their reactions.
- Continue the story:
"Now you are lying in bed. It has been an exciting and exhausting day. Among other things, several sisters and brothers from the church stopped by your shop to comment on the news about Saul. You are resting and neither quite awake or asleep when you have this strange vision. In the vision you are told to go visit Saul so that he can recover his sight."
- Again, ask the class to think about their possible reactions and to record them. Give students one minute to do so.
- Finally, continue the story:
"The vision persists. You decide that it is indeed the will of the Lord that you go visit Saul. You do so. He receives you with both joy and contrition. You pray with him and lay your hands on him. He recovers his sight. Now he tells you that he wishes to join the church. You leave him to go find the other sisters and brothers and tell them that Saul wants to be baptized."
- Ask the class to think about what they (Ananias) might tell the rest of the church. Give students one minute to write down some of their thoughts.

- Invite students to form discussion groups of three persons.
- In these discussion groups, review the various questions, comparing notes, and discussing them. Obviously there will be no right or wrong answers.

Teaching Tip

Your purpose is not to find out exactly what Ananias did, but to get into the story and the tension and conflict behind it in ways that we often miss because we do not stop to think about the implications of what we are reading.

(E) Select persons to be apostles.

- Select three or four students to be the "apostles."
- Ask the apostles to sit in a small group to one side of the room.
- Appoint six "messengers" whose task will be to bring news to the "apostles."
- Ask each messenger to look at a portion of the story and to come and tell their bit of news to the apostles as follows:
—Messenger 1: Acts 9:1-2
—Messenger 2: Acts 9:3-9
—Messenger 3: Acts 9:10-19
—Messenger 4: Acts 9:20-22
—Messenger 5: Acts 9:23-26a
—Messenger 6: Acts 9:27 (Barnabas goes and convinces the apostles)
- As each "messenger" delivers the news to the apostles, the apostles should discuss the message, while the rest of the class members listen. The apostles should remain unconvinced until "Barnabas" brings "Saul" (could be another class member) before them and tells them the story.

(F) Imagine that you have never heard this story.

- Tell students that they are to imagine that they have never heard the story before.
- Read several sections of the story, asking students to suggest possible continuations of the story.
- Insist that students do not know the story, nor do they know that Saul would eventually become one of the greatest leaders of the church. All that they know is what they have read in Acts so far.
- Now read the story, dividing it with opportunities for suggested "continuations" or "endings" of the story. (Encourage people to be imaginative. For instance, when Saul falls to the ground, the "Voice" could "zap" him!) Read the story in the following sections: Acts 9:1-2, Acts 9:3-4, Acts 9:5-9, Acts 9:10-14.

- Provide opportunity for discussion of how our various suggested "endings" or "continuations" differ from the actual story, and how they reflect a different understanding of how it is that evil is overcome. (In our culture, and in human society in general, we often try to overcome evil by destroying the evildoer. God destroys evil by loving, converting, and forgiving the evildoer.)

Dimension 3: What Does the Bible Mean to Us?

The first point made in the study book in Dimension 3 is that true, radical forgiveness is available to us. When God forgives, God erases. The past no longer tugs at us as something to be overcome. It is over and done! You can make this point by using one of the following options.

(G) Connect two concepts.

- Write on newsprint (making the same errors given here): "mary had a litel lamp, its fleas was pink as snow."
- Give the marker to a student. Invite the student to correct the errors.
- After the student has corrected the errors, say that you can still see mistakes. Ask the student to fix it in such a way that all trace of the mistakes is gone. (Obviously, it can't be done. The more you cross the mistakes out, the more obvious it becomes that they were made.)
- Turn the page over. Give the student a clean sheet of paper and ask him or her to write the lines out correctly. (Now it can be done!)
- Read Paul's words in 2 Corinthians 5:17.
- Ask students if they can see any connection between what Paul said and the exercise they have just done. (There being a "new creation" is something like being given a new sheet of paper or "a clean slate.")
- Connect those two concepts (the clean sheet of paper and the passage in 2 Corinthians) with Paul's experience on the road to Damascus and thereafter.
- Ask students to discuss any connection they might see. (For instance, at Damascus, Paul did not have to undo all the evil he had done before he could be baptized and admitted into the community. He was forgiven. That was that. If then he began preaching and teaching, he did this out of gratitude, or out of a response to God's call, but not in order to repay the evil he had done.)

(H) Consider forgiveness.

- Ask:
—According to the text we are studying, what did Paul

have to do so that Jesus would forgive him? (Obviously, nothing.)

—What do you think we have to do so that God will forgive us our sins?

The second point made in the study book is that, just as we have been forgiven—and just as we are constantly being forgiven for new sins—we must also be ready to forgive others. Make this point through the following activities.

(I) Imagine a situation.

- Invite students to imagine the following situation: Your church is in a difficult neighborhood. Years ago, when the church building was put up, this was one of the most affluent areas of town. You can see evidence of this fact as you look at the beautiful stained-glass windows that adorn the sanctuary. As the neighborhood changed, things got tough. Two or three years ago, some of the young people in the neighborhood began throwing stones at the stained-glass windows. The church made a great effort (finances are no longer what they used to be) to put up wire mesh to protect the windows. For awhile, the youth in the neighborhood found other sport. Now some of them have begun shooting bullet holes in the windows. Last week someone shot a hole through a window that your grandparents donated. It made you furious—you had just come from your grandmother's funeral when you first saw the horrible hole in the window.

  You arrive at church early on a Sunday morning. You have the key and are supposed to open the building so that the teachers and class leaders can prepare for Sunday school. You find the door ajar. It has not been forced. Apparently it was not properly locked. You fear what you might find inside.

  As you walk quietly into the sanctuary, you see someone kneeling at the rail. You hear sobbing. You walk quietly down the aisle. You are ten feet away when the praying figure looks up at you. The person is one of the worst thugs who for years has been vandalizing the church!
- Ask: What would you do?
- Provide quiet moments of reflection. Then open up the session for discussion. Whenever it is appropriate (if it is appropriate) connect this situation to the situation experienced by Ananias and Barnabas.

(J) Prepare skits in teams.

- Divide the class into two to four teams and ask each to prepare a short skit. This skit should be about a modern-day Ananias, someone who receives news that an archenemy of the church and of the gospel has been converted, and someone who is now asking that this "Ananias" sponsor him or her in a bid for church membership.
- Tell the teams that they should let their imaginations run through the story, that a bit of humor would not be entirely amiss.
- Have the teams draw aside for a few minutes in order to prepare their skits.
- After a few moments, bring students back together, and have each team present what they have prepared. (Obviously, each skit should be no more than two to four minutes.)
- After all skits have been presented, lead the class in a discussion. As you do so, try to keep that discussion revolving around two themes:
—What does the skit actually tell us about our willingness or unwillingness to forgive?
—Are there any elements in the Ananias story that would help illumine both the skit and our own reactions to people whom we would rather not forgive?

(K) Recall personal wrongs.

- Invite students to think about a person who has so wronged them that they simply could not stand next to that person in church. It could be a business acquaintance, a relative, a neighbor, or any other person they choose. The one requirement is that this person must be one whom they would find difficult to forgive.
- If no one has wronged them so, ask students to think of a person who apparently is so corrupt that there will never be a place for him or her in church. If possible, this person should be someone they know personally.
- Give each student a slip of paper and a pencil.
- Ask students to write the initials of the person or write something else that reminds them of that person.
- Assure students that no one else will see that paper. It is for personal use only.
- When students have written the names of others who have wronged them, tell them to think of all the reasons why they chose that person.
- Ask students to put the paper in their wallet or purse. Whenever they see it, ask them to offer a brief prayer asking two things:
—First, that God will intervene in that person's life and transform it.
—Second, that God will help them forgive that person, just as God has forgiven them.
- Ask students to keep that paper in their wallets for as

long as necessary—at least, until the second part of their prayer has been answered.

(L) End the class with a prayer.

God of love, God of forgiveness, God of such love that you have forgiven even us, give us the love and the understanding to forgive others. In so doing, may they see in us a reflection of your love, and come to you, only source of all love, all forgiveness, and all true life. Through Jesus Christ, whose love was such that he died for us, and whose forgiveness is such that he still loves us. Amen.

Additional Bible Helps

"Saul" or "Paul"?

A statement that is often heard about Paul's conversion is that it was so radical that, before his conversion his name was Saul; then he became Paul. It is true that Paul's conversion was quite radical and dramatic. But that fact has nothing to do with his name. Since it is quite likely that someone in class will bring this up, you will need to have some information on the matter.

That this fact is wrong, the Acts of the Apostles itself shows quite clearly. All you have to do is keep on reading. It is "Saul" who not only got up after encountering the Lord, but also "Saul" who was baptized, who preached in Damascus, who then went to Jerusalem, who fled to Tarsus, who was sought there by Barnabas, and who became a leader of the church in Antioch.

It is only in Acts 13:9 that Luke introduced Saul's other name. He did this with the simple phrase: "Saul, also known as Paul. . . ." The immediate context in which Luke introduced that name is interesting, for Saul/Paul was speaking to a proconsul whose name was also Paul—or as the NRSV translates it, Sergius Paulus.

The fact of the matter is that Paul, like many of his contemporaries, had more than one name. (Note that "Silas" in Acts is "Silvanus" in the Epistles.) As a Roman citizen, he must have had three official names, of which one was Paulus (Paul). It is impossible to know the others.

It was also customary, especially in some of the provinces where other cultures were dominant, for a person to have also a fourth name (in Latin, a *signum*) given at the time of birth. This fourth name was more personal and had more to do with one's particular cultural heritage. Thus, it would appear that at birth this Roman citizen, one of whose three official Roman names was Paul, was also given a Jewish fourth name or *signum*. That fourth, but more personal name was Saul, probably given to him in honor of the first king of Israel and greatest hero of his own tribe of Benjamin.

Thus, the truth is that Paul/Saul would use one of these two names depending on the circles in which he was moving. In the early chapters of Acts, where the context was basically Jewish, he was "Saul." But in chapter 13, where for the first time in Acts Saul was encountering the Gentile world, Luke began calling him "Paul." After that, the only places where the name "Saul" reappeared were Paul's two accounts of his own conversion, where he was obviously quoting the words that he heard in Aramaic, addressing him by his Jewish name.

Conversion

The episode studied in this lesson is usually referred to as Paul's "conversion." It certainly was that. Yet, it may be helpful to clarify the full meaning of the word *conversion*.

As it is used today, *conversion* usually means a change of religion. A Hindu is "converted" to Christianity. A Gentile "converts" to Judaism.

Strictly speaking, in the Bible the verb "to convert" usually has a different meaning. It literally means to turn around and has to do essentially with a change of direction. The Hebrew people, for instance, were repeatedly invited by their prophets to "convert" to God. This may have meant to leave the idols and turn to God. It may also have meant to abandon injustice in favor of God's justice, or to abandon any other sort of evil that God detests and to turn to that which is pleasing to God.

Thus, to say that Paul was "converted" does not necessarily mean that he abandoned Judaism, or that he decided that Judaism was a false religion. He never thought that—not at the time of his conversion, nor even in his strongest passages in Romans or Galatians. Paul was "converted" in the sense that he abandoned a course of action that was wrong and opposed to God's will and turned to a different course of action.

To understand this difference, you may look at other experiences that we often call "conversions." Wesley at Aldersgate did not abandon his Anglican Christian faith, but rather discovered a new dimension of it. In this study, we shall not have the opportunity to look closely at Acts 10; but it has been said that Acts 10 is not only the story of the conversion of Cornelius to Christianity, but also the story of the conversion of Paul to a wider understanding of the scope of the gospel. Likewise, modern chroniclers speak of when Archbishop Romero, while holding the dead body of one of his priests and a friend, was "converted to the poor." What this statement means is not that he abandoned the faith he had held until then, but rather that he discovered a new dimension of it—a dimension so important that it would change his entire life and eventually lead to his death.

This discussion is not to say that one does not have to come to the point where one discovers and accepts Jesus as God's promised Messiah, Savior, and Lord. It is to say that the word *conversion* has many different yet similar meanings. All of these meanings are important, for the Christian life is in many ways a life of repeated "conversion" to the paths of God!

6

Acts 11:19-30; 13:1-3

ℋORIZONS

LEARNING MENU

Keeping in mind the ways in which your class members learn best as well as their needs and interests, choose at least one learning segment from each of the three Dimensions that follow.

Opening Prayer

God our creator, earth has many languages,
but your gospel proclaims your love
to all nations in one heavenly tongue.
Make us messengers of the good news
that, through the power of your Spirit,
all the world may unite in one song of praise;
through your Son, Jesus Christ our Lord,
who lives and reigns with you in the unity of the Holy
*   Spirit,*
one God, now and forever. Amen.

(From *Book of Common Worship.* ©1993 Westminster/John Knox Press)

(A) Reconcile two statements.

● The first two verses of our passage tell how Christianity came to Antioch and how it was that Christians there began preaching to Gentiles. Verse 19, however, seems to imply that Christianity came to Antioch directly from Jerusalem, whereas verse 20 speaks of "men of Cyprus and Cyrene." Ask the class to try to reconcile these two statements.

Teaching Tip

Since there are several different solutions, your goal is not to come to an agreed upon answer, but simply to encourage class participants to read the text carefully.

(B) Note the leadership.

● Focus attention, not on the very early leaders of the church in Antioch, but rather on those who are mentioned at the beginning of chapter 13.

- List the leadership on newsprint or chalkboard.
- Invite class members to answer to the best of their abilities where each of the five primary leaders originated.
- As answers are suggested, point on the map to the places named.
- Write the places mentioned next to each of the five leaders.
- At the end of your work, you should have something like the following:

Barnabas	Cyprus/Jerusalem
Simeon	Cyrene?
Lucius	Cyrene
Manaen	Jerusalem?
Saul	Tarsus/Jerusalem/Tarsus

(C) Name important developments in the church of Antioch.

- Point out to the class that in this passage there are three important developments that took place in the church of Antioch.
- Invite students to name the three developments.
—They began preaching to the Gentiles;
—Antioch was where the disciples were first called "Christians";
—For the first time in the entire Book of Acts a church actually commissioned people to be sent out in mission.

Dimension 2: What Does the Bible Mean?

One of the points we have been trying to make throughout this study, and certainly a central point in the Book of Acts, is that the developments that Acts narrates took place under the guidance of the Holy Spirit. This is important for Luke, since it contradicts any who still bemoaned the fact that the church was rapidly becoming a Gentile community. According to Acts, this was not the doings of humans alone, but of the Holy Spirit, who had guided the church along ever more surprising paths.

This passage, together with the ones referring to Philip and the Ethiopian eunuch, and to Peter and Cornelius, is trying to show that the mission to the Gentiles, begun independently and more or less simultaneously in at least three different places, was the result of the inspiration and guidance of the Holy Spirit.

You may make this point in several ways.

(D) Mark references to the Holy Spirit.

One way to make this point is to say that the Acts of the Apostles are the acts of the Spirit.

- To make this point, take a Bible that you do not mind marking, and, using a good concordance, mark all the references to the Holy Spirit (or to the Spirit) in the chapters in Acts that we have studied to this point (up to 13:3).
- Use a highlighter of a color that will stand out even as you leaf through the Bible in front of the class.
- Now look for words such as *apostles*, *the Twelve*, or individual names such as *Peter* or *John*.
- Highlight those words and names with a marker of a different color.
- Bring the marked Bible to class. Allow participants to leaf through it. Ask whether they think that this book could appropriately be called the "Acts of the Spirit."

(E) Answer questions.

- Select three Bible passages that seem to mark new beginnings in Christian mission and that speak of Gentiles coming into the church:
—Philip and the Ethiopian Eunuch (Acts 8:26-39)
—Peter and Cornelius (Acts 10)
—today's passages, Acts 11:19-30; 13:1-3
- Assign each passage to a different class member or small discussion group, comprised of three to five members.
- Ask them to read the passage trying to answer the question:
—What is the role of the Holy Spirit in this story?
- Tell them you will expect them to make a brief report of their findings.
- After all three have reported, ask participants to imagine that they are Jewish Christian readers who still have some misgivings about the mission to the Gentiles.
—How would they react to these stories and to the references to the Holy Spirit in them?

(F) Combine some elements from the previous two activities.

- Take a Bible and, in each of the three passages mentioned under activity (D), highlight every reference to the Holy Spirit.
- Use this Bible to show the class that all of these various initiatives in mission to the Gentiles took place under the inspiration and guidance of the Holy Spirit.
- Make photocopies of all three passages. Make enough copies so that you have a copy of a passage for each member of the class. For instance, if you have fifteen participants, make five copies of each of the three passages.

- Provide pencils or highlighters.
- Divide the class into three discussion groups.
- Invite each participant within the groups to mark every reference to the Holy Spirit in the passage they have received.
- Instruct each group to discuss what significance they see in the reference assigned to them regarding the Holy Spirit.
—What is Luke trying to tell us about these various initiatives?
—Were they good or bad (according to Luke)?
- Bring the class back together and hear brief reports from each of the groups.

A second point to be made is that the leadership of this church was varied, and that perhaps precisely because it was so varied, it was also very innovative. You may make this point in one of the following ways.

(G) Note again the origins of leaders.

- Look again at activity (B).
- If you did not use that option, do make a list of the five leaders of the church in Antioch.
- Ask students to tell you all they know about the life and background of each of those five leaders to this point.
- As students report their knowledge, underscore their different points of origin—probably all the way from Jerusalem in the east to Cyrene in the West, and as far north as Tarsus. It is clear that most of them were not originally from Jerusalem, although several had some contact with that city.
- Ask:
—Do you think that this variety in their leadership was one of the factors that allowed this church to be so innovative?

(H) Conduct independent research.

- If you have class participants who have the time and the interest to do independent research, assign some of them to study particular issues that may enrich understanding of the various backgrounds of these leaders.
—Someone, for instance, could look up "Cyrene" in an encyclopedia.
—Someone else could look up "Tarsus."
—Another could study about the court of Herod the tetrarch, where Menaen came from.
—Someone could also study the implications of skin color for social relations in the first century, and thus the significance of Simon's being called "Niger." (This will require some specialized and difficult research that will only be possible if you have access to people who have studied such matters.)

The study book indicates that, on the basis of the biblical text, the center of the Christian faith had shifted from Jerusalem to Antioch. Such shifts of centers are not unusual in the history of the church. Since the church lives and grows by mission, it is normal for its life to be more vibrant and creative precisely at those points where the mission is taking place, that is, at the edges. Thus, the edges gradually become centers, only to be replaced in their turn by other growing edges. Naturally, this process is difficult for those who are accustomed to being at the center of things and suddenly must cope with the fact that the center is moving elsewhere.

To present this point to the class, use one of the following activities.

(I) Present a skit.

- Before the class session, work with a small team to present a brief skit. The following roles need to be assigned:
—A missionary who went in 1870 to a land in Africa where there were no Christians. Now there is a flourishing church, the direct result of the work of this and other missionaries.
—Two or three members of the church today, who are firm believers in missions, and who are upset because our church no longer has as many missionaries as it once did in that African nation. The church members should complain about how things have changed, and how we need missionaries like those in old times. After awhile, have the missionary come in and show that they are actually unhappy because the missionary work of earlier generations was successful. In a way, while praising the work and the dedication of those earlier missionaries, they are taking away from their achievements by insisting that the same thing ought to be done all over again. Have the missionary tell about the great things that are happening in that church in Africa under African leadership; how some of the present missionaries are working under that leadership; and, if that is the case, about the missionaries that they are now sending out.
- After some dialogue, when the church members become convinced of what the missionary says, one of the church members should ask:
—In that case, what are we to do today?
—Does that mean that we no longer have a mission?
- The skit participants should openly discuss these questions, while other members of the class listen.

- After some time of discussion among the participants in the skit, invite the rest of the class to join in the discussion, and try to discover what "mission" should mean for our churches today when there are already Christian churches throughout the world.

(J) Present another skit.

- Again, before class, prepare a different skit from that presented in activity (I).
- This skit should involve two people from Jerusalem who are upset about what is going on in Antioch. They are particularly upset because Antioch is sending out its own missionaries, and Jerusalem is losing control.
- The Jerusalem Christians should have a dialogue about what is happening and how it threatens to change the way things have always been done. If possible, let them insert some humor into the situation.
- Tell the rest of the class that they are church members from Antioch. Have them respond to what they have heard the people from Jerusalem say.
- Allow the two from Jerusalem to respond so that you may develop a lively discussion.
- After some time, interrupt the discussion. Share the following information:

> In many ways we may be in the position of first century Jerusalem. For generations, the churches of the first and second world have been a center—perhaps the most important center—of missions throughout the world. Things have changed. There are Christian churches in just about every nation in the world, each trying to fulfill their own mission. At present, third-world Christians are involved in sending missionaries to the nations of the first and second worlds.

- Ask:
—When we complain that things are not as they used to be, is our argument similar to those that we have just heard from these Christians from Jerusalem?

(K) Listen to a resource person.

- In many of our churches or in other nearby places, we have people who are responsible for explaining to the church how the mission of the church is evolving, and what responsible Christians can do in a changing world. Invite such a person as a resource to your class.
- Give the resource person this lesson to read beforehand (both the teacher and the study material).
- Explain that the class is focusing on the Bible and that you will lead the first part of the class, but that during the session you will give this person the opportunity to explain how things have changed and what that means for our missionary responsibility today.

The second point made in the study book suggests that mission is always a give-and-take proposition and that, therefore, Antioch had something to contribute to Jerusalem. Here are some ways to make that point.

(L) Share statistics on the growth of the church.

- Share statistics about the growth of a former mission of your congregation.
- Compare these statistics with others regarding your congregation's growth. (You will probably need to consult your pastor.)
- Ask: Do you think that we might benefit from inviting leaders from the mission to share about their evangelism work?

Teaching Tip

Leaders choosing to use activity (L) should be prepared to spend a good bit of time "digging out" growth statistics. Not every congregation has knowledge of how mission endeavors supported by the congregation have done. For example, many missions in The United Methodist Church are supported primarily through the connectional system of apportionments. Under this system, churches are directly involved in the support of missions but may not be aware of individual mission projects. Additional mission support is carried out through Advance Specials, a system of "second mile" or "advance" mission giving. If you are not able to gather statistics regarding a particular mission of your congregation, revise the activity in the following way:

- Share information about the growth and development of your own congregation. Most pastors will be able to share the statistics of your church with a minimum of effort, but you may want to give your pastor a few days to gather the information. General impressions are fine for the purposes of the lesson.
- Share that third world missions have had phenomenal success, resulting in the sending forth of missionaries to first and second world nations, including our own.

(M) Discuss.

- Discuss:
—Is there something lacking in the life of our church?
—Have you heard of other churches—preferably churches overseas or poorer churches nearby—from which we might learn something?

Finally, the third point to be made in this class is that mission must constantly be evolving, depending on the changing circumstances, and above all because the Holy Spirit is constantly calling us to new adventures of faith.

(N) Discuss the role of the Holy Spirit.

- Remind the class that it was the Holy Spirit who told the leaders in Antioch to set aside Barnabas and Saul for mission to the Gentiles.
- After all that we have learned in this session, ask:
—Do you think that the Holy Spirit may be calling our church to new adventures in obedience?
—What do you think those new adventures might be? (For instance, is there a demographic change taking place in our city or neighborhood? If so, what should our mission be in that context? Or, who are the people in our neighborhood who most need the gospel, and what must we do to bring it to them?)

(O) Read the newspaper.

- Provide three or four clippings from your local newspaper about things that clearly demand an active Christian witness.
- Ask the class to discuss what our response should be. (Examples of such items could be: reports on illiteracy in the community; racial tensions; homelessness; ineffective schools; drug use and sales.)

(P) End the session.

- To end the class, read aloud Acts 13:1-3.
- Remind students that these leaders did what they did in a context of worship, of fasting, and of prayer. If we really wish to discover the will of God for us today, we must put ourselves in a listening mood.
- Ask the class to pray with you:
  God of Peter and the apostles in Jerusalem, God of Paul and the church in Antioch, God of believers through the ages, our God, show us your will, we pray. We know that you have a mission and a purpose for us—for this church and for each one of us. Show us your will. And, if it does not agree with our will, we pray that you will bend our will to yours, so that your will may be done on earth as it is in heaven. Through Jesus Christ, our Lord. Amen.

Additional Bible Helps

Jerusalem Versus Antioch

When we hear that the center of the Christian mission moved from Jerusalem to Antioch, we may be inclined to think that it moved from the great Holy City to a lesser place. That was not the case. In population as well as in wealth, Jerusalem could not compare with Antioch. Indeed, Antioch was the third largest city in the Roman Empire—after Rome and Alexandria—and it had a population of approximately half a million.

It was a beautiful and prosperous city. Sitting on the banks of the river Orontes, just a few miles from the seaport of Seleucia, it could easily carry on maritime trade throughout the Mediterranean. Towards the East, a relatively short distance separated it from the valley of the Euphrates and all the riches of Mesopotamia and beyond.

Thus, Antioch was a place where all cultures and religions met and mingled. For that reason, there were in Antioch many Jews, and they were allowed to practice their religion with little interference from a government that was primarily concerned with trade and order, and not much with religious disputes. There, many Gentiles became interested in Judaism. Some converted to the faith of Israel—as was the case with Nicolaus, that "proselyte from Antioch" who was elected one of the seven in the church of Jerusalem (Acts 6:5).

For the same reason, once Christianity began making headway in Antioch, there was not there the bitter opposition on the part of the more orthodox Jews that we have already found in Jerusalem—and that Paul and Barnabas will meet in many lesser cities. On the contrary, Antioch provided a space in which the new Gentile Christianity could prosper and develop without constantly having to fear persecution on the part of the more traditional Jews.

For generations, until the advance of Islam in the seventh century, Antioch remained an important center for the Christian church and a place where contact was kept between the Greek-speaking Christians of the Roman Empire and the Aramaic-speaking Christians whose missions expanded far towards the east.

The Origin of the Term *Christians*

On the origin of the term *Christians*, you may wish to know (and perhaps to tell the class, if there is an appropriate opportunity for it) that the earliest writing in which the term *Christianity* appears is a letter from a bishop of Antioch early in the second century. Thus, it would seem that both words, *Christian* and *Christianity*, had their origin in Antioch.

7

*J*EALOUSY AND JOY

Acts 13:13-52

LEARNING MENU

Continue to weave a mix of activities and discussion to help students move in rhythm between what the Bible says and how its interpretations and meanings make an impact on each Christian's personal, congregational, and social lives in the world. Choose at least one learning activity from each of the three Dimensions.

Opening Prayer

By the fire of your Spirit, O God, forge us into one church,

many and different people, together in Christ's embrace.

Set our hearts aflame with a love for the truth and the desire to do your will,

that our witness to Christ may burn brightly in lives of joyful discipleship.

Amen.

(Adapted from *Book of Common Worship.* © 1993 Westminster/John Knox Press,1993)

- Point out (if no one else does so) that by the time the missionaries got to Antioch of Pisidia, John Mark was no longer with them.

Teaching Tip

One of the reasons for using the map is to make it clear in a visual fashion that there is a difference between Antioch of Pisidia, where Paul and Barnabas are now, and Syrian Antioch, from which they have come and to which they will eventually return.

(B) List the characters.

- Make a list of all the characters who appear in the story.
- Encourage students to be as exhaustive as possible. Their list should include: Paul, Barnabas, the Jews in the synagogue, the "God-fearers" in the synagogue, the Gentiles in the city, the distinguished devout women whom the Jews recruited, the leaders of the city who expelled Paul and Barnabas, and the believers to whom the last verse refers.
- Invite class members to share as much as they can about each of these people or groups of people.

(C) Note two significant changes.

This initial discussion of the text, joined with the review of what took place in Cyprus, may be enhanced by noting the change that took place in the way Acts referred to the two principal characters in this story.

- Point out that here we have two significant changes:
- —"Saul" had become "Paul." If you did not discuss the significance of the two names when you studied Paul's conversion, this may be a good time to do so. (Look back at what was said about the two names in that lesson. Point out that the change of name took place precisely at the beginning of the Gentile mission and really had nothing to do with Paul's conversion.)
- —The order has now been reversed. Previously, Acts spoke of "Barnabas and Saul." Now they have become "Paul and Barnabas." (In next week's lesson, when we return to Jerusalem, you will note that the order will again become "Barnabas and Paul," for the former was better known to the Christian community in Jerusalem.)

Dimension 2: What Does the Bible Mean?

(D) Write an outline.

- Divide the class into smaller groups, comprised of three or five persons each.
- Ask each small group to write an outline of the history

of Israel before the time of Jesus. Instruct them to use no more than four to six points.

- Allow only a few minutes for writing. Bring the class members back together.
- Ask class members to compare the outlines they have prepared with what Paul said about the history of Israel.
- —Are there things they included that Paul did not mention?
- —Are there things that Paul mentioned, which they did not include?
- —Why do they think that Paul chose these particular items in his retelling of the history of Israel?

Optional Method

- Proceed as with activity (D), but without dividing the class into smaller groups.
- Simply ask the class to list the four to six points in the history of Israel that they consider most important.
- As they mention significant points, write them on the chalkboard or newsprint, keeping them in chronological order.
- After students have completed this task, proceed with the discussion as suggested under Option (D).

(E) Present a skit.

- As you prepare for the class, ask two or three members of the class to prepare a brief skit.
- Ask willing participants to pretend that they are members of the Jewish community in Antioch of Pisidia and to think about what life must have been like trying to remain faithful in that society.
- Point them to the material in their study book, pages 57-58, which outlines some of these difficulties, and encourage them to use their imagination as they prepare a skit in three acts.
- —The first act is to take place in the living room of a participant. Skit participants should comment about how difficult it is to remain a faithful Jew in the setting in which they must live. Encourage them to invent an incident on which they may be commenting. (For instance, one of them may be about to lose a profitable contract because he won't work on the sabbath. Or another may be commenting about how difficult it is to bring up children who remain faithful to their traditions in a society in which all the other children are constantly going to religious festivals of various kinds.)
- —The second act is to take place in the same living room, after that first session in the synagogue at which Paul and Barnabas spoke. They are all excited about what they have heard, and they are commenting on what this news might mean for their lives.

—The third act is to take place again in the same living room, but now after the second sabbath, when they have seen their synagogue inundated by Gentile pagans. They are quite upset. Have them express the reasons why they are so upset. Again, encourage them to use their imaginations. In the end, they decide that they must not allow Paul and Barnabas to speak in the synagogue again, that they must warn all faithful Jews against them, and that they must find ways to get rid of them.

(F) Focus on Barnabas.

Since Barnabas was less important in the narrative as Paul came to occupy the center of the stage, this would be a good opportunity to focus for a moment on Barnabas and his character.

- Ask a member of the class to prepare for this session by looking up the name of Barnabas in a concordance and listing all the facts that we know about him.
- Give the reporter an opportunity to report to the class. (Besides what we know from the Book of Acts, other information appears in Paul's Epistles.)
- Lead the class in a discussion of Barnabas and what we can learn from him and his story.
- Make sure that his positive traits are made clear: his generosity in selling his property and giving to the needy; his openness in accepting Paul and presenting him before the apostles; his willingness to give Paul a position of leadership, even though Paul would eventually overshadow him.
- Make sure that some of his conflicts with Paul also come out: their disagreement as to whether to take John Mark with them on their second missionary journey and the harsh words that Paul said about him in Galatians.
- Note that, in spite of these differences, Paul continued showing love and respect for Barnabas.

Teaching Tip

Your purpose in using this method is to show that Barnabas was great precisely in that he, who was a leader, was also open to the leadership of others. Also, although he had serious differences with Paul and made no attempt to ignore or hide those differences, the two remained united in a common purpose.

(G) Write a brief history of your congregation.

- Divide the class into small work groups.
- Instruct each group to write a very brief outline of the history of your congregation. This outline should have no more than six points—preferably less. Allow only a few minutes for this exercise.
- Bring the class together. Invite each smaller group to compare notes with other class members. (Provide newsprint so that each group can write their outline and then post it up for all to see.)
- As class members compare results, lead them in a discussion asking:
—Why did we mention these events and not others? (The point is to try to discover how we envision ourselves. Of what are we proud? Are there things we would rather forget? It is also to point out that in any congregation there are people who have different memories and that all of these memories combined make up for our common identity.)
- At the end of the discussion, relate this exercise to the manner in which Paul told the story of Israel and how his own perspective and purpose helped determine the events he chose at least on two points:
—By emphasizing the role of King Saul, who was a member of Paul's own tribe and also had the same name;
—By emphasizing the message of John the Baptist, since this was a perfect introduction to the point he wanted to make about Jesus.

(H) Present a skit.

- Ask two or three members of the class to prepare a skit before class. The skit will have three acts, all to take place in the living room of one of the participants in the conversation. Ask them to imagine that they are members of a congregation that has a long and distinguished history. They have been members for a long time (some of them since birth, for their ancestors were brought up in this church). They will need as a prop three calendar pages, with dates three to four years apart.
- Encourage participants to use their imagination and to create concrete examples and cases of which they are speaking in their skit.
—The first act, with a calendar page in the background, will have these people talking about their church. They are to show that they are proud of their church and all it has done in the past. They must also indicate how difficult it is to be faithful to the tradition they have

received. It is difficult to cover the budget, especially with all the expenses connected with the upkeep of facilities. Society is changing, and people are no longer as helpful to each other as they used to be. So many people are looking after their own interests that it becomes increasingly difficult to be loving to each other. Few are willing to volunteer for the many tasks that need to be done. Yet, these people in your skit will show that they are proud of their church and that they are particularly proud that they are remaining faithful even in the face of all these difficulties.

—The second act takes place a few years later (indicated by a different page on the calendar). The same people are talking in the same living room. Now there is a new excitement about their church. New people are coming in! The choir has new voices. There is a renewed evangelistic zeal. Although some members have moved away from the community, the church is having a greater impact among recent arrivals. There is new life.

—The third act (again in the same living room and with a different calendar page) takes place still a few years later. Now the same people are angry. The new life in the church was O.K. for awhile. But now things have gone too far. The newcomers are taking over everything. They have even begun to change some of the furniture around. (Again, encourage the actors to let their imaginations run.) It seems necessary to put a stop to things. Otherwise the newcomers will take over "their" church. Have them discuss what they are going to do. (Perhaps, for instance, they will agitate to have the pastor changed. Or they will talk to others who feel the same way, then see how they can limit the influence of these new arrivals.)

- After the skit, lead students in a discussion as to whether they see any connection between the skit they have just seen and the Bible passage we are studying.
- At the end of the discussion, if it seems appropriate, ask students:

—Do you see any parallels between the situations we have discussed and our own situation?

(I) Discuss how inviting you are to newcomers.

- Relate the role of welcoming newcomers to Barnabas' role in welcoming Paul into the fellowship of the church in Jerusalem, then going to fetch him from Tarsus to Antioch of Syria. Relate the attitudes some Christians share today to the attitude of the Jews in Antioch of Pisidia, who apparently welcomed a number of "God-fearers" as long as there were not too many of them.
- Lead students in a discussion of how we invite and welcome newcomers into our church.
- Use the following questions as an outline:

—Are we a welcoming church?

—Imagine that you came to worship in our church for the first time. Would you feel welcome? What would give you that feeling?

—Or would you feel unwelcome? Why?

—If you were here for the first time, would you guess that people would make you feel welcome *before* they asked your name, what you do, or where you live?

—If you looked different from the rest of us (in dress, in race, in age, or in any other way), would you feel equally welcomed?

—As you look around our worship service, do you see new people? If so, who are they?

—Are any of them different from the majority of us?

—Are they a fair representation of the community within a radius of a mile around the church?

—If not, what can we do to invite and to welcome those segments of our surrounding community that apparently do not feel that our church is for them?

—If we are a welcoming and inviting church for all people, or if we were to become one, what difficulties follow from that inviting and welcoming spirit? (We are not to believe that welcoming new and different people into our fellowship is easy. If we think that there are no difficulties, we deceive ourselves, and the result will be that we will not be a truly evangelistic, inviting and welcoming church. It is best to be realistic about this possible dilemma, and then to tackle with faith and creativity whatever difficulties might come up.)

(J) End the session.

- End the class with a prayer:
  God, our creator, we are mindful of the many mercies and privileges we have received from you. To these we ask that you add the grace to share these mercies and privileges with others, and that we welcome others into our family of faith, as you have welcomed us into your family. In the name of Jesus, our Lord and brother. Amen.

Additional Bible Helps

Distinctions Within Paul's Speech

Paul's speech began by addressing two groups, "you Israelites," and "others who fear God." In normal usage, the first category would probably include, not only those who were Jews by birth, but also proselytes—Gentiles who had decided to join the people of Israel through circumcision and full obedience to the law. The second group, which you have already encountered in other lessons, would consist of Gentiles who, while accepting the basic monotheistic and moral tenets of the faith of Israel, were not ready to join Judaism in all its ceremonial and dietary dimensions. Such people would be present at this gathering of the synagogue, although they would not participate fully in the service. The same distinction appears at the beginning of the second part of the speech, where Paul addresses: "you descendants of Abraham's family," and "others who fear God." From these two instances, it would seem that there were in the synagogue these two groups, easily and clearly distinguished from each other.

The problem is that at the end of the story (in verse 43), Luke introduced language that complicated the issue. In verse 43, a difficult phrase appears. The NRSV translates it as "many Jews and devout converts to Judaism." The problem is that the word that the NRSV translates as "devout" was used most often to refer to the "God-fearers," whereas here it refers to the "converts"—or, in another translation, "proselytes." (Actually, if you look at verse 50, you will note that there the "devout women" are precisely what could also be called "God-fearing women.") Some scholars have suggested that the original text in verse 43 said only "devout," and that "converts" was added by a later copyist. That solution has found little support among students of Acts. Most likely the truth is that Luke used the term *converts* (or *proselytes*) more loosely than usual, meaning both actual converts and people who believed the faith of Israel but were not ready to take the step of a formal conversion.

A Positive Tone

You may note that this speech does not have the strong anti-Jewish flavor of others we have read in Acts. Remember, for instance, Stephen's speech, where he spoke repeatedly of Israel's disobedience (a theme, in any case, which was not the creation of Christian anti-Jewish sentiments, but which Judaism itself had incorporated in the writings of its prophets). In this speech, addressed to Jews outside of Jerusalem, who therefore had nothing to do with the religious elite that had opposed Christianity from the beginning, Paul was quite positive about Israel's history.

The one point at which a slightly more critical note appears is verse 18, where he said that for about forty years God "put up with them in the wilderness." Yet, not all manuscripts say even that. Others say, in a much more positive tone, that God "cared for them" in the wilderness. (In Greek, the difference is very slight, and the two words may be easily confused.)

The reason for this more positive tone is obviously that Paul was speaking to people who had nothing to do with the events in Jerusalem and was addressing them as himself a Jew, telling them that the promises by which they had always lived are finally being fulfilled.

A Radical Turning Point?

The declaration in verse 46, "we are now turning to the Gentiles," has often been interpreted as if this were a radical turning point, after which the missionaries decided that the Jews would not believe and so turned only to the Gentiles. Although this particular declaration is crucial in understanding the process that Acts describes, Luke did not mean to say that from this point on the mission was confined solely to the Gentiles. On the contrary, as you continue studying the Book of Acts, you will note that in most cases the first contact that Paul made in a new city was through the synagogue. For instance, the very next chapter records that "the same thing happened in Iconium, where Paul and Barnabas went into the Jewish synagogue and spoke. . . ."

The entire story of what happened in Antioch of Pisidia is not to be read as a turning point, but rather as an example of what must have happened in place after place as Paul and others went about preaching the gospel. Their natural point of contact was the synagogue. Furthermore, Paul and Barnabas, as well as other Christians, were convinced that what they were teaching was not some new religion, but the fulfillment of the promises made to Israel, which were central to the Jewish faith.

8

Acts 15:1-35

JERUSALEM

Opening Prayer
> *God of wind, word, and fire, we bless your name this*
> *day for sending the light and strength of your Holy*
> *Spirit.*
> *We give you thanks for all the gifts, great and small,*
> *that you have poured out upon your children.*
> *Accept us with our gifts to be living praise and witness*
> *to your love throughout all the earth;*
> *through Jesus Christ, who lives with you in the unity of*
> *the Holy Spirit, one God, for ever. Amen.*

(Don E. Saliers. From *From Ashes to Fire*, page 248; © 1979 by Abingdon)

Dimension 1:
What Does the Bible Say?

(A) Reflect on study book questions.

- Looking at question 1 in the study book (page 61), ask participants to list the cast of characters and to state briefly the role that each of them played in the entire story.
- From this point you may wish to move directly to activity (C) under Dimension 2. In that case, you will want to list the cast of characters on the board or newsprint as they are mentioned by various members of the class.

(B) Trace Paul's movements on the map.

- Using the map, ask class members to trace the movements of Paul, as Acts describes them to this point. Tack down the length of ribbon or yarn used in previous sessions, noting Paul's movements.

- Referring again to the map, but not tacking down ribbon or yarn, note the travels of Barnabas and of Silas. (For instance, at the beginning of the story Barnabas was in Jerusalem. Then he went to Antioch; to Tarsus to fetch Paul; and back to Antioch. With Paul, he went on that first missionary journey to Cyprus and then to Antioch of Pisidia, Iconium, and so forth. He was back in Antioch when he was named part of the commission to go to Jerusalem. At the end of our passage for today, he was in Antioch.)

Optional Method

- Instead of presenting this material yourself, or asking the class to try to reconstruct these itineraries, talk to two participants before the class.
- Invite one to reread the Book of Acts to this point in order to trace the movements of Paul.
- Ask the other participant to follow the same instructions to research Barnabas. (Silas had not appeared in the narrative before today's passage, and therefore there is no need to ask someone to trace his earlier movements.)
- You may wish to assign someone to use a concordance and find out as much as possible about Silas. In that case, explain to that person that "Silas" is also "Silvanus," who appeared with that name in the Epistles of Paul and Peter.)

Dimension 2:
What Does the Bible Mean?

(C) State the position of the characters.

- On the basis of the cast of characters that you listed in Dimension 1, activity (A), ask the class to note the position of each of the participants (or group of participants) in the meeting in Jerusalem.
- Through a process of discussion, help the class clarify the issues that were at stake. List these on newsprint or chalkboard.
- List also on chalkboard or newsprint any main positions in conflict.

(D) Dramatically read the Bible text.

- Assign one class member to each of the three following roles: PETER, a Pharisee who insists that Gentiles who become Christians must obey all the law; JAMES; the "SECRETARY" of the meeting.
- Read aloud the passage.
- As you come to the words pronounced by the Pharisee (5), point to the person playing this role. This participant

should then read what the Pharisees said.
- Repeat this process for the words of Peter and for James.
- When you come to the letter, have the "secretary" read it aloud.

(E) Roleplay the passage.

- This method is a revision of activity (D). No script is used.
- Assign two persons to be Paul and Barnabas in addition to the other characters mentioned under Activity (D). (No one was assigned the roles of Paul and Barnabas in the previous activity, because in this passage Acts did not quote them directly, but simply summarized what they said.)

(F) Debate a question.

- Prepare and conduct a debate on the question: "All Gentile converts to Christianity must obey the law."
- Assign two people to defend that position, as would have the Pharisees to which the text refers.
- Assign two others to defend the opposite position. (If you wish, these two others could be characters in the story, such as Peter and Paul.)
- Keep the debate short. Give each person two minutes to present arguments for their position, and a half minute at the end to try to refute what the other side has said.
- Participants may need a little coaching beforehand, in particular to make certain that the "Pharisees" understand their role and their position.
- After the debate, open up the session for discussion.

(G) Explain the stipulation about blood.

- One of the things that some people find confusing about this passage is that today most Christians do not obey the stipulations about not eating blood. It is difficult to present this point by any other method than a straightforward explanation. Share the following information.

What was being decided was not, strictly speaking, the principles by which Gentile Christians had to live. Rather, what was being decided were the minimum principles Gentiles had to follow in order to keep communion with Jewish Christians. James' stipulations (as noted in the study book, page 64) were a summary of the ancient laws for aliens living in the midst of Israel. For James and for the rest of the church in Jerusalem, the church was essentially a Jewish movement; the question was how these aliens in their midst could be part of their communion, and how they could accept them, without themselves breaking the law and becoming polluted. Thus, as the church became less and less Jewish and more and more Gentile, these stipulations lost their importance. (Obviously, to this day Christians accept and try to follow the first two stipulations about idolatry and fornication.)

- If your class could profit from further clarification, you may wish to use the materials that appear in the Additional Bible Helps section. This further information will help explain that, as the church became increasingly Gentile, there were those who began interpreting the stipulations of Jerusalem as a moral code, which was not the original intention. (This was the reason why the reference to "things strangled" was dropped. This text became the basis for speaking of the three "great" sins: idolatry, fornication, and homicide.)

Dimension 3:
What Does the Bible Mean to Us?

(H) Consider the Council at Jerusalem.

- As an introduction to this dimension, review what is said in the study book, page 65, regarding the reason for the different attitudes of the Pharisees in Jerusalem, and of Paul, who was also a Pharisee.
- In this discussion, invite the class to review what we have learned about Paul's career and development since the time of his conversion. Consider the possibility that some of the events that Acts narrates may have contributed to bring Paul to the position that he now held with reference to the law and the need to obey it. For instance, think about the story of what happened in Antioch of Pisidia, and how the Gentiles showed an openness to the gospel, which many of the Jews did not show.
- Ask: How did Paul's experiences lead him to the position that he upheld at the Council at Jerusalem?

(I) Consider how events change our perspectives.

If Paul and many others in Acts grew in their understanding of the faith by being involved in mission (think, for instance, of Peter in his encounter with Cornelius), it is quite possible that some members of the class may have similar experiences to report.

- Ask willing participants to share personal testimonies. (The writer of this guide will never forget the day a fellow student in high school came to him and asked him what the Christian faith was all about. Justo had heard the story and its meaning since childhood. He believed the story and believed himself to be a Christian. But it was in telling another student the story and seeing the change that it brought about in him, that Justo gained a much deeper appreciation for the story and a stronger commitment to it. As a result of that conversation, both students grew in the faith, and eventually both became pastors.)
- If the members of your class are likely to offer such testimonies spontaneously, you may plan to do so in the session itself.
- You may also know of some particular experiences that members of the class have had, in which they have grown in the very act of witnessing. If so, you may wish to approach these persons before the class and ask whether they would like to tell about their experiences in this regard.

(J) Learn about the "Tale of Two Churches."

- Suggest the possibility that class members read this first half of the Book of Acts as "A Tale of Two Churches and Two Cities." Indeed, much of this part of Acts revolves around Jerusalem and Antioch and the churches there. Share the following in the form of a "mini-lecture":

A Tale of Two Cities

Jerusalem is the old center of Judaism. For Judaism Jerusalem was not only the center of religion, but also in a sense the center of the world. Indeed, much of what the prophets had promised as the glorious fulfillment of the promises of God had to do with all the nations coming to Zion. The church there was a very active and creative church. In the early chapters of Acts we saw how that church persevered in prayer and in the teaching of the apostles, and also how they shared with each other so that there was not a needy person among them. We also saw that they were innovative in their response to new situations, as in the case of the problem posed by the distribution of support among the widows of the Hebrews and the Hellenists (chapter 6). Furthermore, they were a rapidly growing church, for at several points in those early chapters of Acts, Luke told of the large numbers who joined the church or who believed and were baptized. It also had an ideal cadre of leadership—no less than the apostles themselves, the people who had been trained for leadership by personally following Jesus in his earthly ministry.

Yet this large and flourishing church soon lost its position of leadership in responding to new situations. This is clearly seen in the passage we are studying, where although the church in Jerusalem still had the authority to decide what was to be done, it was Christians from Antioch who took the lead in opening up the practice that Jerusalem then sanctioned. This was all the more surprising for, as the result of the experience of Peter with Cornelius, the church in Jerusalem had a glimpse of the new situation, and of what the new policy would have to be. Apparently, it lost that glimpse over the years, to the point that it had to be reminded by the delegation from Antioch.

In contrast, Antioch was a very different city. To begin with, it was a cosmopolitan place where Jews would never be as comfortable, for they always had to be in contact with Gentiles and found it difficult to keep their ritual purity. It also was a much larger city than Jerusalem, with wider contacts throughout the Mediterranean world as well as towards the East. Therefore, we should not be surprised that it was a city of innovation, where all sorts of strange ideas coexisted with sound creativity.

The church in Antioch responded well to that situation. It too was a creative and innovative church. Its leadership, although not able to boast of the "pedigree" of those in Jerusalem, was varied, coming from different parts of the world and probably from a wide variety of experiences. Therefore, it is not surprising that it was in Antioch that proclaiming the gospel to Gentiles became a generalized practice. Nor is it surprising that it was in Antioch that the believers were first called "Christians." Finally, it is not surprising that it was from Antioch that the first missionaries were sent, and that the mission to the Gentiles began.

In the long run, the church in Jerusalem lost its position of leadership. When there was a Jewish revolt against the power of Rome, the small Jewish Christian remnant in Jerusalem fled to Pella. Eventually they returned. But the Christian church in Jerusalem remained small, conservative, and increasingly isolated from the rest of Christianity.

Meanwhile, the church in Antioch flourished. By the second century it was recognized as one of the leading churches in the entire world. It sent missionaries, not only toward the West, as we read in Acts, but also toward the East. Eventually, that action led to an expansion of Christianity that reached as far as India and China.

"A Tale of Two Cities": we see that contrast summarized in the contrasting attitudes of Paul, the Pharisee from the church in Antioch, and the reactionary Pharisees from the church in Jerusalem.

- Ask:
—To what extent are we like the church in Jerusalem?
—To what extent are we like the church in Antioch?
- Lead the class in a discussion on this subject. The following subquestions or themes may help you in this task:
—How does the city (or if you wish, the culture) of which we are a part consider itself the center from which the rest of the world must learn?
—If that is the prevailing attitude in the society around us, is this an attitude shared by our church?
—Do we presuppose that we are to teach and lead the church into the rest of the world? Or are we a church that is willing to learn from other churches—say, churches in Zimbabwe or Brazil?
—No matter where we are set, it is clear that our society is becoming more diverse and cosmopolitan. Understandably, there are those in our society who feel threatened by these changes and who seek to resist them. What is our attitude in the church?
—Do we see these changes as a threat to our traditional position of leadership?
—Do we welcome them as an opportunity for mission?
—Is our church responding creatively to these changes? Or is our church continuing in its traditional practices, hoping that things will again be as they used to be?
—What are some signs that our church is engaged in mission, both to those far away and to those in our own community who are different from most of us?
—What have we learned from that missional outreach?
- Conclude this discussion with a show of hands where class members express personal opinions as to whether your church is more like Jerusalem or like Antioch. (Or you may give them the opportunity to "hedge" their vote by asking them to vote for a number from one to ten, where one is most like Jerusalem and ten is most like Antioch. Add the votes and average them.)

(K) End the class session.

- End the class session with a prayer:
Dear and loving God, we confess that we prefer our traditional settings to new and challenging surroundings, and that as a result we are often not as engaged in reaching others as we should be. We need your strength

and guidance to venture from our own securities and go forth in your mission, especially to those who are or seem to be different from ourselves. We pray for that strength, and for the vision that must go with it. In the name of Jesus, who left the comfort of his throne to be one of us. Amen.

Additional Bible Helps

Difficulties in the Passage

One of the main difficulties of this passage is to relate it to what Paul himself said about this and other related incidents. In Galatians 2:12 for example, Paul spoke of an incident that is quite similar to the one we are studying. He said that the people who went to Antioch from Jerusalem "came from James," that is, that James sent them. Acts said nothing of the sort. Furthermore, in the same passage in Galatians, Paul said that Peter ("Cephas," as Paul called him in his Epistles) was already in Antioch, and that he was quite willing to eat with the Gentiles until James' representatives arrived. Apparently Paul was quite angry, for he added that "even Barnabas was led astray by their hypocrisy" (Galatians 2:13).

Furthermore, the order of events as told in Galatians was somewhat different than what appears in Acts. In Galatians, Paul spoke of a visit to Jerusalem that he made in the company of Barnabas and Titus. According to Paul, he went to Jerusalem "in response to a revelation." During that meeting, he met in private with "James, Cephas, and John, who were acknowledged pillars" of the church in Jerusalem. An agreement was reached whereby Paul would go to the Gentiles, and the others to the Jews. It was after that visit (Paul does not say how long) that Peter came to Antioch, where he was quite willing to eat with the Gentiles until James' envoys arrived. Thus, the debate in Antioch about whether Gentile converts had to be circumcised and obey all the law took place *after*, and *not before*, the meeting in Jerusalem.

Obviously, if one looks at details and tries to take both accounts (Luke's and Paul's) as literal and orderly descriptions of what actually took place, the two accounts are irreconcilable.

How, then, are we to reconcile the two? Probably the most likely explanation is that what we have in Acts is the "telescoped" story of a debate that may have taken a long time to settle, and in which there were several comings and goings, as well as several harsh encounters. In the end, as both Paul and Luke said, an agreement was reached. It was to underscore that final agreement that Luke had both Peter and James speak of in his account, for these were precisely the two that would have been remembered as having clashed with Paul on these matters.

Thus, what Luke actually gave us was the end result of the debate, while sparing us many of the details and in particular some of the uglier confrontations. In the end, Peter, James, Barnabas, and Paul all came to an agreement as to the mission to the Gentiles. In essence, that is what we learn from the letters of Paul—although we learn also that the agreement was preceded by a painful process of debate and confrontation.

The Significance of a Footnote

Perhaps some class participants will note that in some Bibles there is a footnote indicating that the phrase "what is strangled" (20) is omitted in some manuscripts both in James' speech and in the final letter sent by the church in Jerusalem; and these persons may ask about the significance of that footnote.

There are in fact many manuscripts that omit that reference and then add a form of the Golden Rule. The results are the following four stipulations, which you may wish to compare with those that are listed in the study book:
(1) that they abstain from things polluted by idols;
(2) and from fornication;
(3) and from blood;
(4) and from doing unto others what they would not have done unto themselves.

The difference seems slight, but it completely changes the meaning of the "Jerusalem Decree." Having eliminated the reference to "whatever is strangled," the entire decision can be read as having to do with moral rules, rather than with the dietary laws of Israel. If this other reading is correct, then abstaining from "blood" does not mean not eating blood, but rather not committing homicide.

This text, thus altered, became the reason why very soon some Christians made a list of the three worst sins—some would even say "unforgivable sins": idolatry, fornication, and homicide.

In fact, as was explained in the study book, the "Jerusalem Decree" was no moral legislation, but simply a reaffirmation of the ancient laws of Israel regarding aliens who lived in their midst. What those aliens had to do then, in order not to threaten the purity of Israel, these new "aliens"—the Gentiles who had become Christians—had to do now in order to be part of the same family of God with the actual descendants of Abraham. That is why very soon, as the church became increasingly Gentile, these rules were abandoned or relaxed. (In that regard, see Paul's instructions in 1 Corinthians 8:1-13, where he in fact said to the Corinthian Christians that there was nothing wrong in eating meat sacrificed to the idols as long as their doing so did not become "a stumbling block" to those who did not understand this freedom.)

9

Acts 17:15-34

A THENS

Opening Prayer

O that the world might know the all-atoning Lamb!
Spirit of faith, descend and show the virtue of his name;
* the grace which all may find,*
* the saving power, impart, and testify to humankind,*
* and speak in every heart.*

(Charles Wesley, 1746. From *From Ashes to Fire*, page 248; © 1979 by Abingdon Press)

Dimension 1: What Does the Bible Say?

(A) Refresh your memories.

- Through questions and answers, refresh students' memories. Ask:
—Why was Paul in Athens? (He had been forced to flee from Beroea.)
—What was he supposed to be doing while he was in Athens? (He was to wait for Silas and Timothy to join him.)

- Underscore the fact that Paul apparently did not go to Athens with a missionary purpose. On the contrary, Athens was intended to be a temporary stop while the missionary team regrouped. Yet, Paul's own zeal, and the particular circumstances in Athens, led to an entirely different result.

(B) Map Paul's journey.

- Using a large wall map, discover the location of Athens. Note also Beroea from where Paul had escaped.
- Students may want to note these locations on maps within the study book, page 112.

(C) Identify feelings.

- Provide newsprint and markers or chalkboard and chalk.
- Working as an entire class, identify feelings that Paul might have had in escaping from Beroea. Ask:
—What might Paul have felt as he escaped Beroea and ended unexpectedly in Athens?
- Note the feelings suggested and list them for class members to refer to later in the session.
- Ask:
—When you feel the feelings you have identified, what do you want to do? Run away? Hide? What?

Dimension 2:
What Does the Bible Mean?

(D) Share information about Athens.

If there are students who have taken any courses on ancient history or philosophy, or who otherwise may know something about Athens, give them the opportunity to bring their knowledge to bear on the passage we are studying. You can do this in several ways:

- If there are those who have traveled to Athens, and have slides, videos, or other views of the cities (particularly of its ruins) speak to them beforehand, and set aside five or six minutes for them to show these materials. Make certain that they know something about the significance of what they are showing so that this does not become simply a travelogue but can help the class understand something of what Athens was like in the first century. (For instance, if they show a picture of the Parthenon, their comment should not be: "There we are in front of some ruins," but rather: "These are the ruins of the Parthenon. This was one of the main temples of Athens on its highest place. It was dedicated to the goddess Athena." Perhaps they could even add something like: "It is called the Parthenon because that means the temple of the virgin, and the goddess Athena was a virgin.")
- If there are those who have studied philosophy, even at an elementary level, ask them to prepare a brief explanation about the nature of Stoicism and Epicureanism. (Or let them read what is said about those two schools of thought in the Additional Bible Helps.) Give them also a very brief time (no more than a few minutes) to present that explanation.
- If there are those who have studied ancient history, or are interested in it, ask them to prepare a brief outline of the history of Athens up to the first century. They should show in particular that Athens still retained much of its fame and splendor, but no longer had the political and economic importance of former times.

- OR, if you have people in class who enjoy doing a bit of extra research, and who are good at presenting their results in brief and interesting fashion, assign to them any of the three tasks outlined above. For instance, instead of bringing their own pictures they could use pictures from library books or travel brochures, then present and explain them in class. If you assign the third task, they could look up "Athens" in an encyclopedia, or read about it in a history book.

Teaching Tip

Although it would not be quite as effective, since it would not involve class participation at the same level, you may choose to research these concerns yourself and present them to the class.

The value of this exercise for the class will be to help them connect what they read in the Bible with what they have learned from "secular" education or travel. Too often these things are left unconnected to the point that we forget that the Athens that Paul visited was the same city about which we studied in high school or in college. The result is not only that those connections are not made, but also that we do not learn to make parallel connections for our own time. When we learn to read the Bible as if it had nothing to do with its historical setting, we also tend to read it as if it had nothing to do with our own setting. In this particular case in which issues of the relationship between faith and culture come to the foreground, making such connections will help the class begin to think in terms of the relationship between their faith and the culture in which they live and of which they are a part.

(E) Diagram a summary of the situations in Athens.

- Read aloud verses 16-18.
- Invite students to list the various sorts of people that became Paul's interlocutors in Athens and to list where he addressed each of these groups.
- Ask:
—Which of these various interlocutors are new or represent new challenges?
- As the discussion proceeds, diagram a summary on a chalkboard or newsprint. Write what is new in caps and what repeats what we have already seen elsewhere in small letters.
- Toward the end of the discussion, your diagram may read something like this:

Situations		
Jewish presence (verse 17)	IDOLATRY (verse 16)	CURIOSITY (verse 21)
People addressed:		
Jews and devout persons (verse 17)	WHOEVER WAS THERE (verse 17)	EPICUREANS AND STOICS (verse 18)
Where addressed:		
Synagogue (verse 17)	MARKETPLACE (verse 17)	AREOPAGUS (verse 19)
What said:		
Argued (verse 17)	ARGUED (verse 17)	LONG SPEECH (verses 22-31)
Results:		
Not said	NOT SAID	REJECTION (verses 32-33)
		CONVERSION OF DIONYSIUS AND DAMARIS (verse 34)

- Once you have this sort of diagram on the board, it will become quite clear that Acts underlines what is new. We are not told what Paul said in the synagogue, because that would be similar to what he said in Antioch of Pisidia and elsewhere. The emphasis was on Paul's speech at the Areopagus, because there he was encountering a new situation, and Luke's policy throughout the Book of Acts was to give us only that information necessary to move the story forward.

(F) Make photocopies of Paul's speech.

It is difficult for the English reader to catch the irony in Paul's speech, because we do not see the connection between words such as *unknown* (verse 23) and *ignorance* (verse 30). In Greek they are essentially the same word. Thus, Paul began speaking of the Athenian's religiosity and their altar "to the unknown" God, and ended by using the same as proof that the Athenians were themselves "unknowing." What follows is a suggested way to make this point clear:

- Make photocopies of Paul's speech, bring them to class, and distribute them among the participants.
- Tell students that the Athenians prided themselves on their knowledge, and ask them to underline words such as *unknown, ignorance,* and the like.
- Tell students that in the Greek language these words are the same.
- Instruct students to look again at Paul's speech. Share the following information:

Paul took the inscription "to an unknown god" as an acknowledgement of Athenian ignorance, an idea which would no doubt have rankled many listeners. He told them that *he* knew this God whom they did not know, and proceeded to tell them that the manner in which they worshiped was further sign of their ignorance. He came to his conclusion by telling them that there was a way out of their ignorance—an ignorance that would not excuse them at the time of judgment. That way out of ignorance and judgment was Jesus, whose mission God warranted by raising him from the dead. With this news, Paul's listeners decided that they had heard enough. To them, the notion of a resurrection from the dead was the height of folly. And this man who spoke of their ignorance was proclaiming precisely such a resurrection! He was the one who was truly ignorant and foolish! They mocked him; he left.

Dimension 3: What Does the Bible Mean to Us?

(G) Watch religious programming.

The first point that the study book made in this Dimension is that Paul could have been successful had he tailored his speech to what his audience wanted to hear. He did not do that. Thus, in a sense his speech was a failure; but it was a success in the deeper sense that he was faithful in his proclamation.

- One way to present this point would be to videotape some of the most popular religious programs on television during the week. Choose to show a vignette from one or two shows (do not use more than five to seven minutes.)
- As students watch, they are to ask themselves:
—Why is this program such a favorite?
—What does it offer that people seem to want?
—Is what is said and done faithful to the gospel?
—Is something omitted, perhaps because that is not what people want to hear? If so, what?
- Invite students to share responses in small discussion groups of three to five members.
- Return to a large-class format.
- Encourage discussion groups who wish to share highlights of their discussion with the larger class to do so.
- Clarify that your purpose is not to say that all televised religious programming is bad or unfaithful—not even that these specific programs are particularly bad. Your purpose is to train yourselves to analyze what you see and hear in the name of the gospel, to see whether it is indeed a proclamation of the gospel.

(H) Explore temptations.

It is important to see that we are often tempted to be less faithful in order to be more successful.

- Ask:
—Is this statement true of you? "I am often tempted to be less faithful in order to be more successful or more popular."
- Provide opportunity for any who wish to respond with a personal experience.

(I) Discuss the phrase *from one*.

One of the points made in the study material is the importance of verse 26, which affirms that God made all nations "from one."

- Share information regarding the meaning of this phrase, as gleaned from the Additional Bible Helps section of this leader's guide, page 47.
- Discuss your findings.

Teaching Tip

If students object that the story of Adam is not historically true, point out that, quite apart from the physical origin of humanity, it is true that we are all one species—as is becoming increasingly evident as genetic research progresses. You may also wish to mention that, mathematically speaking, any one of us is at least a sixty-fourth cousin of any other person we might meet anywhere on earth.

(J) Explore origins of racism.

- Share the following information:

> Some time ago, a distinguished theologian declared that strictly speaking, racism is not the result of race. The opposite is closer to the truth: race is the result of racism.
>
> What he meant is that as we look at the spectrum of humankind, there is no clear line of demarcation where one race begins and another ends. The lines are much more blurred than that. Physical traits change almost imperceptibly from region to region, in such a way that one cannot really say that a race ends here, and there another begins. Furthermore, the definition itself of a race depends on the society itself. Why is it, for instance, that in the United States a person who has three white ancestors, and one African-American ancestor, is considered black? In other societies, such a person would be considered white.

- Having explained this point, ask:
—Do you think that this man was right?
—Is race more the result of racism than vice-versa? Why? Why not?

(K) Simulate racism.

- Illustrate the point of activity (J) by preparing pieces of paper with consecutive numbers, 1, 2, 3, and so on up to the maximum number of participants in class.
- Give a number to each person, beginning with number 1, and going as high as necessary so that each participant has a number.
- Instruct participants: "The people with the low numbers, please go to my right. Those with the high numbers, please go to my left." (The result will be confusion. Some people (numbers 1 and 2, for instance) will immediately know where to go. Those in the middle will not know what the instruction really means.)
- After the necessary pause so that the confusion sinks in, explain that race is something similar. There are no clear lines of demarcation between races. We construct those lines in order to classify people, and quite often in order to include some and exclude others. But, as Paul says, we are all made from one.

(L) Explore variety in the church.

- Ask:
—If there are all these varieties of people in God's creation, but all are really one, shouldn't our church reflect the variety around us?
—Does it? If not, why not?
—Do we think we ought to change this situation?
—How could we do it?

(M) Consider the care of the earth.

- Share:
—Regarding verse 26, the study book raises the issue of the care and distribution of the earth. For many Christians, these are frustrating issues, for while we know that they are important, we hardly know where to begin tackling them.
—Perhaps a good place to begin would be examining our own patterns of consumption and waste. We tend to think that industrial waste is the greatest and worst of all pollutants. But the truth is that we too pollute the earth by our overconsumption and our own waste.
- Ask:
—Do you think that we could reduce the amount of waste we produce in our own homes if we really tried?
—What could we do to reduce waste? (Some examples are recycling, purchasing less that is really unnecessary, composting, donating used items to charity, and so forth.)
- You may make this a long-term project by asking the class to figure out how much waste they produce in a week (for instance, in terms of how many garbage cans); then challenge them to reduce this by a certain percentage.

- Move to larger issues by asking questions such as:
—When we support a company by buying its products or by investing in it, do we take into account how responsible they are in the management of earth's resources? Should we?
—Are there some products we have decided not to buy or consume because they destroy God's creation? (Tobacco products? Wasteful plastic products? Disposable products?)

(N) End the session.

- Depending on the emphasis you have given to the class, you may wish to end with the singing (or reading of the words) of one of the following hymns:
—"God of the Sparrow God of the Whale," (*The United Methodist Hymnal*, No. 122);
—"O God of Every Nation," (*The United Methodist Hymnal*, No. 435);
—"O God Who Shaped Creation" (*The United Methodist Hymnal*, No. 443).

Additional Bible Helps

Epicurean and Stoic Philosophers
The mention of the Epicurean and Stoic philosophers is quite realistic, for at this time these were the two strongest philosophical schools in Athens. Although the Academy that Plato had founded still existed and flourished, it had been eclipsed by these two other philosophical schools.

Both the Stoics and the Epicureans were essentially concerned with the same question: How does one live wisely? They answered this question in radically different ways.

The Epicureans held that pleasure is the ultimate goal of life. Originally, this did not mean senseless, exaggerated pleasure, which ultimately produces pain. It meant the measured, rational pleasure that avoids excesses and thus prolongs itself. There are no higher moral standards than pleasure and well-being. Eventually, many so-called Epicureans used this philosophy as an excuse for self-gratification and indolence. Therefore, already at the time of Paul this philosophical school was becoming discredited.

The Stoics held that there is a rational principle that permeates the entire universe. All is structured and functions according to this universal reason, which results in a universal or natural law that governs, not only physical phenomena, but also all of life. This means that the wise life is that which is attuned to that natural law. To resist this law is useless, and therefore the Stoic's ideal stage is one in which one really does not care whether one suffers or has pleasure, for both are subject to natural law that one cannot really resist. Virtue consists, first of all, in obeying the natural law; secondly, in submitting to it when it causes us pain or discomfort.

For these reasons, the Stoics were highly regarded as people of high moral standards, and Stoic philosophy was rapidly gaining adherents in the Roman Empire. (By the next century, a Roman emperor, Marcus Aurelius, would be an adherent of this philosophy.)

Areopagus
You will note that the NRSV says that Paul spoke at the Areopagus, while sometimes it is said that he spoke on "Mars' Hill." That is because the name "Areopagus" means "Hill of Ares." Since Ares was the Greek god of war, he soon was equated with the Roman god of war, Mars. Therefore, it became customary to refer to this hill, as "Mars' Hill." In essence, the two names mean the same.

There is some debate among scholars whether the Areopagus to which Acts refers is the hill itself or the council of that name, which in early times met on the hill, and at a later date met elsewhere. The fact is that in Paul's time the council may still have been meeting on the hill. In any case, the nature of the discussion does not seem to indicate that this Areopagus was a council meeting. Such meeting usually had to do with trials, and there is no indication here that Paul was accused or was being tried at all. In fact, when there was disagreement as to his teachings, he simply left. Therefore, the most likely interpretation is that Paul was invited to meet with a group of philosophers at the Areopagus—that is, on the hill—to address them on philosophical matters.

"From One Ancestor He Made All Nations"
The Greek text literally says "from one he made all nations" (26). The NRSV has introduced the word *ancestor* in order to clarify the meaning. There are a number of ancient manuscripts that say "from one blood he made all nations." The problem with the NRSV translation is that it implies that Paul was necessarily referring to Adam. He may have been or he may not have been. All that the text says is that all humankind has a single origin. One could also interpret it as meaning, for instance, that God made all humankind from the same earth. In any case, Paul's point was the unity of all humankind.

Dionysius the Areopagite and Damaris
At some point in the fifth century, a pious Christian of strong mystical tendencies wrote a series of books, giving himself the name of "Dionysius the Areopagite." Since it was thought that this was Paul's direct disciple, these books had widespread impact throughout the Middle Ages, until more careful scholarship proved that they could not have been written in the first century. Thus, when historians refer to "Dionysius the Areopagite," or more commonly to "Pseudo-Dionysius," what they mean are these books and their unknown author. The fact is, we know no more about Dionysius or Damaris than what is in Acts 17:34.

10

Acts
18:1-17

$\mathcal{C}$ORINTH

LEARNING MENU

Choose at least one activity from each Dimension, keeping in mind the learning methods that seem to work best with your class members. Once again, encourage students who have not reflected on Dimension 1 study book questions, to do so as they arrive in the class. Potential answers to questions will be reviewed in activities (A) and (B) below. Prior to class, invite students to research material for activity (C). Use the Additional Bible Helps section of this guide as a source.

Opening Prayer

Gracious God, transform our timid lives by the power of your Spirit,
and fill us with a flaming desire to be your faithful people,
doing your will for the sake of Jesus Christ our Lord. Amen.

(Adapted from *Book of Common Worship.* ©1993 Westminister/John Knox Press)

Dimension 1:
What Does the Bible Say?

(A) Focus on Dimension 1 questions.

● As an introduction to the text, focus the attention of the class on the first of the questions asked under this Dimension, regarding the attitude of Roman authorities toward Christianity. In order to do so, ask:

—What Roman officials are mentioned in this story? (Most probably participants will immediately speak of Gallio. Remind them that at the beginning of the story, in verse 2, Emperor Claudius is also mentioned.)

● Focus on the second question, regarding Paul's means of support. (If participants have read their books, some may suggest the possibility that, although at first Paul supported himself by working full-time as a tentmaker with Priscilla and Aquila, when Silas and Timothy came from Macedonia, they brought with them funds that allowed Paul to devote himself to preaching and arguing with those who opposed the gospel.)

(B) Review Paul's relationship to synogogues.

- Take as your starting point question 3 in the study book, regarding Paul's relationship to the synagogue in Corinth.
- Ask the class to reflect on material studied in previous class sessions. Try to recall Paul's relationship to synagogues in other cities.
- Ask participants to compare what happened in Corinth with what took place elsewhere.
- Outline responses on chalkboard or newsprint:
—Paul preached in the synagogue, and at first he was generally well received, or at least there was no significant opposition.
—Eventually opposition arose. Paul had to find an alternative to the synagogue.
—Finally, violence ensued.
- Add one significant difference in this case:
—We are not told that Paul had to flee from Corinth (see verse 18) just as he did not come to Corinth fleeing from Athens.

Dimension 2: What Does the Bible Mean?

(C) Share the results of student research.

- Before the session, invite two participants to research information about Claudius and Gallio. Since they will only have a minute or two to make their report, research need not be extensive.
- Allow reporters approximately five minutes to share information with the class.
- Ask:
—On the basis of what little we know, what do you think was the attitude of each of these two officials toward Christianity? (Eventually, neither of the two wanted to deal with it. Claudius simply expelled the lot from Rome. Gallio threw the case out of court, then allowed a violent near-riot to develop right at his doorstep.)

Teaching Tip

Part of your purpose in using a "research and report method" is to continue a theme that was seen in the last session: Luke entwined his story in Acts with what was taking place at the time in secular culture and history. Therefore, you may wish to move on to a discussion on how Claudius' decree resulted in Paul having the opportunity to meet Priscilla and Aquila.

(D) Gather research on main characters.

- Provide a few Bible dictionaries, commentaries on Acts, and concordances to the class.
- Instruct participants to make a list of all the characters in the story. The list should include: Paul, Aquila, Priscilla, Claudius, Titius Justus, Crispus, Gallio, and Sosthenes.
- Divide the class into as many groups as the number of characters listed. (Do not count Paul, for we know so much about him that the exercise would be impossible to complete in the amount of time given.)
- Assign one character to each group. Give groups five minutes to find out as much as they can about their character, using the books at hand.
- Bring the groups together. Invite each group to report on what each discovered.
- After all the reports have been made, ask the class:
—Did this exercise make the text come more alive for you?
—Has this exercise piqued your curiosity? Do you want to learn more?

Teaching Tip

Your purpose in doing this research is to give the class a taste of the value and joy of studying the Bible using such tools as Bible dictionaries, concordances, and commentaries. If students appear to have enjoyed this method, plan to use it again in future sessions.

(E) Connect "Corinth" with Paul's letter.

- If members of your class have a fair acquaintance with the Bible, ask them to look at what their books say about Corinth and try to connect this information with what they remember of Paul's letters to the Corinthians.
- Aid in their recollection by mentioning to students the apparent moral disorder of some members of the church in Corinth.
- Ask:
—Have you visited any large seaports with bars and places of gambling and prostitution at practically every corner?
—If so, does your visit help you understand something of the atmosphere in Corinth?
- Mention the problem of the impact of pagan religion, the question of meat sacrificed to the idols, and the various understandings and doubts about the resurrection. Relate this to some of our modern prosperous cities, where all kinds of religions and traditions meet, and where Christians must deal with the question of what their faith requires.
- Consider our most prosperous cities, which include extremes of wealth and poverty. Remind participants of how Paul had to deal with such disparities in the church. Remember that one of the problems at Corinth was that

when they came to Communion, some brought their own food, so that they had a feast while others had hardly anything to eat.

- Finally, remind students that Paul in 2 Corinthians insisted that the Corinthians, who apparently shared some of the wealth of the city, must share wealth with the poor in Jerusalem.

Teaching Tip

Part of your purpose in this activity is to whet the appetite of the class for the study of Paul's letters to the Corinthians, which will come up soon in their journey through the Bible. Enabling students to discover that Christians continue to "battle" with some of the same issues as did earlier Christians may help students appreciate the timeliness of Paul's writings.

(F) Consider Paul's vision.

In verses 9 and 10, Paul had a vision in which the Lord assured him of his safety. This does not seem to come at a time of particular stress or difficulty. In some ways, it may have prepared Paul for his appearance before Gallio's tribunal; but when it came, there seemed to be no particular need for such a word of reassurance.

- Ask:
—Why do you think this vision came at this particular point? (Obviously, there is no correct answer. Some may relate it to Paul's declaration in 1 Corinthians, that he had gone to the city in weakness and with fear and trembling. Some may see it as preparation for the confrontation with the Jews and with Gallio.)

Dimension 3:
What Does the Bible Mean to Us?

(G) Consider how political decisions are made.

Since the study book focuses on the question of how Christians should relate to civil government and its power, begin this section of the class where that material ends. There, you will find listed several bases on which people make political decisions.

- Invite participants to open study books to pages 81-83.
- Read the various options on page 83.
- List options on chalkboard or newsprint.
- Invite the class to list other bases on which one may decide, for instance, to vote for a particular candidate. (Criteria may include someone I know; someone who is a Christian; someone who is trustworthy; someone who is tough on crime; and so forth.)

- Ask students to rank these various criteria on the basis of how important they *should* be for a Christian. (You may do this by a simple show of hands.)
- Ask:
—Are the principles we use when determining our political actions the same as those that we have ranked as of highest importance for Christians?
—For instance, if there was an election recently, were these the criteria that we used in determining for whom to vote?
—Or, if there will be an election soon, are these the criteria we are employing as we come to a decision?
—If the criteria for our decision do not match what we say should be most important for Christians, why is that?
—What can we do to make our voting and other political actions conform more to what we believe as Christians?

(H) Discuss quotes.

Some time ago, the book *The Culture of Disbelief*, by Stephen Carter (Harper Collins, 1993) created quite a bit of controversy. Its main thesis is that in our culture we have trivialized religion, and that doing so is, in part, the result of a mistaken interpretation and application of the constitutional principle of separation of church and state. Carter, himself an active Episcopal layman, argues that the result is a domestication of religion, which deprives it of its power, and also deprives society of the critique and dynamic creativity of religion.

- Read the following quotes. Lead the class in a discussion about them; then ask the questions that follow.

"A religion . . . is not simply a means of understanding one's self, or even of contemplating the nature of the universe, or existence, or of anything else. A religion is, at its heart, a way of denying the authority of the rest of the world; it is a way of saying to fellow human beings and to the state those fellow humans have erected, 'No, I will *not* accede to your will' " (page 41).
—As you read the whole story of Acts, and in particular the story we are studying today, do you think Paul would have agreed with such a statement? Why? Why not?
—Do you agree with this statement? Does your faith ever lead you to resist or reject rules or principles by which the rest of society lives?
—Have you known personally or through books and other media Christians whose faith led them precisely to the sort of resistance that is implied in this quote?

"To insist that the state's secular moral judgements should guide the practices of all religions is to trivialize the idea that faith matters to people" (page 38).
—What do you think Paul would have to say about this statement? What would you have to say?

"Some critics of religious power suggest that the wall of separation is being breached, that religions are gaining too much influence in governance. But the breach, if it exists, also runs the other way, for government may be gaining too much influence over religion" (page 146).

—Is this statement true?

—Where can you see the influence of government over religion? Carter further suggests that one of the ways in which this system functions is through an accommodation in which the state offers tax exemptions to religious organizations, which in turn does not ask hard questions about the way society organizes its life.

—Is this statement true? Does our church compromise its message in exchange for a position of respect or acceptability in our society?

Optional Method

Point out that in the Book of Acts the church existed beyond the margins of accepted society and was often persecuted for that reason. Give the class an opportunity to review some of the episodes that illustrate this fact (the trials of Peter and John before the Council, the death of Stephen, the repeated beatings and flights of Paul and his companions, and so forth).

Obviously, things have changed. What have we gained in the bargain? What have we lost? How can we reclaim some of what has been lost?

(I) Reflect on "tentmaking ministries."

● Although this is not a matter that was brought up in the study book, you may wish to spend some time on Paul's "tentmaking ministry." This passage tells us that when Paul visited a place such as Corinth, and had no other means of support, he simply worked at a trade and then used his free time to preach.

● Share the following information:

In more recent times, there has been much discussion in different churches throughout the world of the possibility of a "tentmaking ministry"—and in fact, many churches have developed such a ministry. The phrase refers to a group of people who are ordained ministers and who perform the functions that are usually assigned to such ministers, but who support themselves at their own trade or business.

Although the reasons often mentioned in support of such a program are financial, there are other reasons that are also given. Obviously, the financial reason is that in this manner churches who could not otherwise afford to pay a pastor have the benefit of one. The other reasons are that this method allows for an ordained ministry that is freer from financial pressures on the part of the congregation. And, in many cases, it is also argued that such ministers, because

---

their lifestyle and means of livelihood are closer to those of their average members, can understand their situation more readily.

● Ask:

—What do you think about such ideas?

—Have you ever known a "tentmaking" ordained minister?

—Do you think there is a place for such a ministry in our church?

—What do you imagine would be the benefits?

—What would be the negative results?

● If you have chosen any of the other options offered above, and have therefore engaged with the class in an exploration of the relationship between faith and culture, and between church and state, you may wish to relate the results with the present discussion. Ask:

—Do you think that the manner in which salaries in the church are established today reflects the practices of corporations and other employers around us?

—If so, what are the values and advantages of having such a system?

—What are the dangers?

—Does this mean that the church has become too much like the society around it?

—Can you imagine any other options?

(J) End in song and prayer.

● End the class session by singing or reading the hymn "For the Healing of the Nations," (*The United Methodist Hymnal*, No. 428).

● Pray:

God of truth and love, you have put us to be witnesses to your truth amidst a nation where there are many different people with different opinions and values. Help us to be faithful witnesses to your truth, while at the same time loving even those from whom we differ the most. We pray in the name of Jesus the Christ, in whom we have seen your Truth and met your Love. Amen.

Additional Bible Helps

Claudius' Decree of Expulsion
We know of this decree from Roman historian Suetonius, who says that Claudius "ordered Jews to leave Rome because they were constantly producing turmoil at the instigation of Chrestus." Most historians agree that "Chrestus" was "Christus." The reason for the expulsion, they believe, was that, as in so many other places, Christian preaching caused division among the Jews, and that such divisions led to riots that Roman authorities would not condone.

It is not clear whether literally "all Jews" were forced to leave the city, or only those who had been involved in the riots. In any case, the date of the decree was the year A.D. 49, and a very short time after that there certainly were Jews living in Rome.

Aquila and Priscilla

This couple became close collaborators with Paul, who declared that they "risked their necks for my life," and also that for them "all the churches of the Gentiles" give thanks (Romans 16:4). They left Corinth with Paul when he went to Ephesus, and there they corrected the preaching of Apollos, who in spite of all his eloquence seems to have been defective in his theology (Acts 18:24-28).

The study book says that probably Priscilla was a more important leader in the earlier church than Aquila. The reason for this is that most often their names appear in that order: "Priscilla (or Prisca) and Aquila." Since, as we have seen, Luke is rather careful in such matters, and at that time order of naming usually indicated also order of importance, it would seem that Priscilla was usually thought of as the leading force in this couple's commitment to the Christian faith. (The fact that Luke refers to her by the familiar diminutive form of her name, "Priscilla," would seem to indicate that he knew her personally, or at least that he had heard of her from a tradition that felt deep affection for her.)

Romans 16 would seem to indicate that Priscilla and Aquila eventually returned to that city, where one of the ancient catacombs is known as the "Cemetery of Priscilla." Also, at least as early as the fourth century there was in Rome a "Church of Saint Prisca"—which by the eighth century had become the "Church of Saints Aquila and Prisca." Still later, probably in the tenth century, somebody wrote the legendary "Acts of Saint Prisca." (Recent excavations under that church have uncovered an aristocratic house from the first century that may well have been Priscilla's. This, and other reasons, have led some to suggest that Priscilla was a member of an aristocratic Roman family. If so, this was an example of a phenomenon that became quite common in early Christianity: a cross-class marriage.)

Paul's Tentmaking

It is not clear what it was that Paul actually did in connection with tents. It has been suggested that he wove the heavy cloth made of goats' wool that was sometimes used for making tents. Another possibility is that he made tents out of such cloth. But at that time many tents were also made of leather, and therefore it is also possible that Paul was some sort of a leather worker.

Gallio and the Dating of Paul's Sojourn in Corinth

Lucius Junius Gallio Annaeus was a native of Spain and a brother of the famous philosopher Seneca. Like Seneca, he was a friend of Nero, who helped Gallio further his political career. Eventually, both Gallio and Seneca fell out of favor with Nero, who ordered them to commit suicide.

We know that Gallio was proconsul of Achaia (the province whose capital was Corinth) from July 51 to July 52. (The post of proconsul of a province was normally held only for a period of one year.) Based on this fact, and on the date of Claudius' decree expelling the Jews from Rome (A.D. 49), it is safe to assume that the time that Paul spent in Corinth was approximately from the fall of 50 to the spring or summer of 52. This is one of the few episodes in Acts that is possible to date with a fair degree of accuracy. The date of Gallio's proconsulship was not known until certain archeological discoveries early in the twentieth century helped determine it. Yet, the fact that it matches perfectly with the date of Claudius' decree shows that, in general, Luke has fairly good control of his facts.

Sosthenes—Official of the Synagogue

This verse (17) is puzzling, among other things, because some manuscripts say that it was "the Greeks" who beat Sosthenes. It is also puzzling because its very obscurity leads one to think that at least some of Luke's intended readers would have known quite readily who this "Sosthenes" was. This would seem to imply that he was a Christian, and one fairly well known in early Christian circles.

There may be a clue in 1 Corinthians 1:1, where we are told that this Letter, written from Ephesus to the Corinthians, is being sent by "Paul, called to be an apostle . . . and our brother Sosthenes." Thus, there was a Sosthenes who was known to the Corinthian church, and who may well have been the one who received a beating in front of Gallio's tribunal. If so, he may have left Corinth for Ephesus at about the same time as Paul. Still, the question remains, why did whoever do the beating attack Sosthenes, and not Paul? Again, this is a question that is impossible to answer.

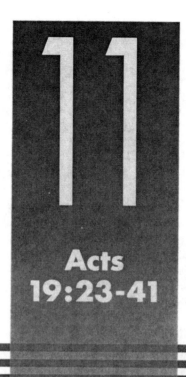

11

Acts 19:23-41

$\mathcal{E}$PHESUS

LEARNING MENU

Again, keep in mind your class of learners and how they best learn. But surprise them a little too—and they may well surprise you! If you discover students are not reading the passage in their Bibles and writing out answers to the Dimension 1 questions at home before class, suggest that they read the passage and answer the questions when they first come into the classroom. Encourage students to work together. Provide another option for students who have already dealt with Dimension 1 questions.

Opening Prayer
"The love of God has been poured into our hearts through the Holy Spirit that has been given to us" [Romans 5:5]. Thank you, O God, for the gift of the Spirit. Empower us to see clearly this day, the Spirit's works in our lives and in the lives of your followers long ago. Amen.

Dimension 1:
What Does the Bible Say?

The three questions under this Dimension in the study book would suffice to guide you in a study of the entire passage. Yet, since what you wish to do is simply to use this initial approach as a way to whet the appetite of the class for further study, you may wish to limit yourself to either learning activity (A) or (B).

(A) Ask a question.

- Ask the first question:
—Who instigated the riot, and why?
- Allow for some brief discussion about this question, so as to get the class to review the story in their minds, and then move on to the next Dimension.

(B) Engage in map study.

- Connect this week's passage with last week's. Use the maps in the study book, or refer to the map in the *Bible Teacher Kit* (Abingdon, 1994) entitled "Paul's Journeys." The latter map is a large wall-sized map you may want to refer to often in subsequent sessions.
- Help students see that, after the episode in Corinth that was studied last week, Paul has completed his second major missionary journey. The third journey is about to begin. Help them see also that this was not Paul's first visit to Ephesus after his conversion, for during his return from his first missionary journey he stopped in that city.
- Trace on the map the locations visited by Paul on various journeys. Ask:
—Why do you suppose he seemed to visit some of the locations more often than others?

(C) Dramatize events.

- Invite students to dramatize the story.
- Before class, prepare name tags as follows: "Demetrius"; "silversmith" (2); "town clerk"; "Gaius"; "Aristarchus"; "Paul" (optional); "disciple" (2, optional); "Asiarch" (2, optional); "Alexander"; "Ephesian rioter" (enough for all the rest of the class).
- Distribute the nametags to willing participants.
- Give each student a moment to read the story once again, and (if they are participants in the drama) to see their role in it. If they wish, they may also look in the study book (or, in the case of the Asiarchs, in the Additional Bible Helps in this leader's guide) in order to get more information or possible ideas about their roles.
- For the drama, the class leader should assume the role of the narrator and read the story as it appears in Acts.

Teaching Tip

At each appropriate moment stop to allow the "actors" to perform their parts as they best can. (You may need to signal one or two of them that this is their cue to come in, and encourage some by asking questions or making suggestions.) Adults learn well from participating in roleplays IF laughter and fun are a part of the effort. Keep it lighthearted and informal.

- Begin with a meeting between Demetrius and the silversmiths. In the drama, Demetrius should attempt to get the silversmiths riled up about Paul's preaching and its possible consequences.
- All three should then attempt to convince another person in the class to join them. That person should attempt to convince another, and so on, until all but those who have been assigned special roles have joined the "riot."
- Encourage these people, as they call each other, to join them in the march toward the theater, to confuse the issues, and to simply agree on the chant or shout, "Great is Artemis of the Ephesians!"
- Along the way, have them meet Gaius and Aristarchus, recognizing them as Paul's followers.
- If time permits, Gaius and Aristarchus may wish to try to defend themselves. The rioters should not allow any such explanations.
- If you wish, and depending on how you plan to distribute the time allotted for the class, invite "Paul" to decide that he is going to the theater in order to face his accusers. At that point invite first the disciples, then the Asiarchs, to give reasons why he should not go.
- Continuing with the drama, return to the theater.

"Alexander" should attempt to put in a word, explaining that, although he is a Jew and does not worship Artemis, he is not like Paul and his followers. The rioters should pay no attention to him and shout him down.
- Finally, the town clerk should attempt to explain his position, and the position in which this incipient riot is placing the entire city. He should be explicit about the possible consequences of what they are doing.
- In the end, the rioters should calm down and quietly sneak back to their chairs.

(D) Research items of interest.

- As in previous lessons, invite one or two members of the class to research (in advance) some items that may be of interest and will help us understand the passage we are studying. In particular, have them find out what they can about the city of Ephesus and its history, particularly during the first century.
- Students researching information will find a good Bible dictionary, such as *The Interpreter's Dictionary of the Bible* (Abingdon, 1962) helpful.
- Those who have researched information should be allowed ample opportunity to share about Ephesus and the temple of Artemis/Diana during the session.

(E) View a video.

- The ruins of Ephesus are among the most visited ancient ruins in the eastern Mediterranean. Therefore, if you have access to the *Bible Teacher Kit* (Abingdon, 1994) this would be an excellent time to view the third section of the video, "Places Paul Visited" (11.46 minutes). This segment vividly shows the ruins of Ephesus, while providing a quick look at other locations visited by Paul on various journeys.
- If you do not have access to the video, see activity (F).

(F) Invite a resource person.

- If you do not have access to the video mentioned in activity (E), perhaps someone in your class or community has visited the Holy Land. Ask him or her to share slides or talk with the class members about the area. Offer this person ten or fifteen minutes of class time to share information or artifacts that may be of interest. (The most interesting remaining ruin in Ephesus is the theater itself. Of the temple of Diana, there only remains one column, and few tourists visit it.)

Teaching Tip

Visit your church library or pastor's study for resource books on Ephesus, if you cannot use either activities (E) or (F). Many atlases, Bible commentaries or Bible dictionaries may feature photographs of the ruins.

(G) Discover common themes.

- Invite the class to discuss Paul's stay in Ephesus.
- As part of your discussion, identify themes students find in this section of our study, which have been themes in previous sessions, as well as emergent new themes. (For example, one common theme would be the good beginning in the synagogue, and the eventual separation from it. A significant difference would be that here the major opposition did not come from Jews who refused to accept the gospel, but rather from Gentiles who saw their businesses threatened.)
- Ask the class:
—Can you recall another incident in Acts where Paul encountered opposition from people whose economic interests he had hurt?
- Tell the class that there is one such incident participants should have encountered, although it is one that they will have encountered in their Daily Bible Journey and not in the passages we have studied in depth. (The passage in question is Acts 16:16-24, where Paul and Silas were imprisoned because Paul had healed a young girl from a "spirit of divination" that produced much gain for her owners. It is interesting to note that most people remember the episode of Paul and the jailer in Philippi, but few remember why Paul and Silas were in prison in the first place!)

Dimension 3:
What Does the Bible Mean to Us?

(H) Identify with main characters.

One way to deal with this passage is to place ourselves in the position of different characters in the story and, from those positions, see what the text tells us. To follow this option, you may do the following:

- Begin with **Demetrius and the silversmiths.** Here were people with definite economic interests who convinced themselves that what they were doing, they were doing for the glory of Artemis. Ask:
—Is there any possibility that we may, in some cases, do something similar? (Remember that, as was said in the study material, it is possible to be quite sincere and still fall into the trap of the silversmiths.)
- Ask the class to consider the following:
—Several decades ago, H. Richard Niebuhr published a book called *The Social Sources of Denominationalism,* in which he showed that denominations in the United States are separated and distinguished by social class and social traits more than by theology or even by polity or practice. The same could be said of individual congregations within a particular denomination.

—Why is it that we belong to this particular denomination and/or this particular congregation?
—Does it have to do with the "kind of people" whom we meet in church?
—Have we chosen this particular church because the people in it are those with whom we feel most comfortable?
—What is it that really distinguishes us from other churches in the area?
—Do we actually confess to ourselves that these are our real distinguishing characteristics, or do we deceive ourselves with all sorts of explanations about our particular theology, our form of worship, or our form of government?
- Still under the heading of Demetrius and the silversmiths, you may consider another approach. Share:
—In many of our churches and denominations there is a constant debate between those who think that evangelism is more important than justice issues, and those who think the opposite. In truth, the Bible does not place these two in opposition, but rather tells us that it is impossible to do evangelism without acting justly and promoting justice. When Christians work for justice they must do so while proclaiming the good news. Still, we make these distinctions and pit one against the other.
- In this context, ask:
—Why might we say that our concern should be only for evangelism, and that we should leave aside issues of justice?
—Are there hidden agendas (hidden even to us) that we must discover and confess?
- Ask the opposite question:
—What hidden agendas might persons have, who speak often about justice but not about the saving power of Jesus Christ?
- Examine the role of the **rioters.** They joined the silversmiths, without really stopping to think and to learn what it was all about. They heard that their goddess was threatened, and they joined the crowd.
- Ask:
—Can you think of any instances when you have done the same? (If the class itself does not suggest such cases, you may suggest one or two possible examples. One may be what many of us have done with the new theologies coming out of the third world. We read someplace that they are inspired in Marxism, and assume, therefore, they are really communist theologies. Are we among those who have passed on this word, without ever stopping to read one of the works of these theologians?

Another example may be the comments some of us have heard and passed on about denominational policies and decisions. For instance, suppose the church issues a document for study on a controversial subject. Soon some group or another comes out condemning what "the leaders of the church are saying." Do we take the time to verify matters before we pass on what we have heard? Do we distinguish between what someone or some agency has issued as a subject for discussion, and what their actual position may be?)

- Use these examples to reflect on the possibility that, at some points, we may act like those rioters in Ephesus.
- Ask the class to imagine that they are **Gaius and Aristarchus**. Ask:
—Have you ever been in a position (perhaps in the workplace) where, no matter how hard you might have tried, your Christian witness was not heard?
- Imagine Gaius and Aristarchus there in the middle of the riot.
—From what sources do you think they could draw strength for that difficult situation? prayer? the community of the church that they knew was with them?
—From where do you draw your strength in difficult situations?
- Finally, ask the class to place themselves in the position of the **town clerk**.
—Have you ever been in situations in which you seemed to have some authority, but in reality had to follow the will of someone else?
—What do you do in such a situation? Hide the limits of your own authority? Hide behind the authority of those above you? Look for compromises?
- Again, if the class does not come up with its own suggestions, offer an example:
—Imagine that you are the president of a college that has a very prestigious drama department. Every year half of the town comes to see the plays that the department puts on. This year the department wants to put on a controversial play about tobacco as a business and as a threat to health. You are in the middle of tobacco-growing country and much of your money comes from donors in the area. How do you decide what to do? (Your purpose in asking this question is to help the class realize that in daily life ethical matters often present themselves as dilemmas. As Christians we have to practice how to make ethical decisions in such situations.)

(I) Explore how Paul dealt with Roman authorities.

- Lead a discussion in which you examine, first, the manner in which Paul dealt with the Roman Empire.
- In that process, share:
—While it is true that the Roman Empire suppressed many liberties, it is also true that it gave many people an opportunity to live in relative peace and prosperity. Paul was a Roman citizen, and he used that citizenship on occasion, although not to show any superiority or authority over other believers. Paul counseled obedience to authority, and specifically to Roman authority; still, Paul knew

where he had to stand firm, and eventually was killed by the same Roman authorities to whom he had counseled obedience. We live in a society that has produced prosperity such as the earth has never seen. It is also a democratic society with powerful democratic institutions. At the same time, it is a society deeply in need of reformation so that people whom it excludes may be included in its prosperity and freedom. It is a society whose impact on other societies has sometimes been very positive and sometimes rather negative.

- Ask:
—Is it possible that for us also, as for Paul, there may be some elements or policies in our society that are difficult to reconcile with the gospel?
—If so, what is our attitude toward them?

Teaching Tip

The purpose of this discussion is to look at our society and the powers within it with something of the complexity and sophistication with which Acts looks at Ephesian society and the powers at work within it. This may be a very difficult discussion for some classes or individual participants. Engage in such discussions with great sensitivity. Encourage diversity of opinion, as well as respect for such diversity. As adult learners trust the care in which discussions of sensitive matters are shared, they may become more open to sharing diverse opinions.

(J) Write a contemporary version of the story.

- Provide pencils and paper.
- Invite participants in small groups of three to five to write a contemporary version of the story studied in this session. Tell them that the only rules are that it has to be set here, in our time and general neighborhood, and that each story has to have characters corresponding at least to the following biblical characters: Demetrius, the silversmiths, and the town clerk (they can add others as they wish).
- Allow ample time for students to reflect and write contemporary stories.
- When students have finished, invite those who are willing to share their stories with the larger group.

(K) Pray.

- End the class with a prayer:

God in heaven, above all the gods that we make for ourselves, help us to serve you and only you. Cast out the false gods that we make for ourselves—the gods of money, prestige, and success—just as you did cast out the ancient gods that people made for themselves. In the name of Jesus, your true Son, our Lord. Amen.

Ephesus

Ephesus was an ancient city, whose origins disappear into antiquity—probably the twelfth or thirteenth century B.C. It was on the river Cayster, whose mouth provided an excellent harbor. Since ancient times, however, the harbor was often obstructed by silt deposits, and today the ruins of Ephesus are some five miles away from the sea. It was part of the kingdom of Pergamum when King Attalus III died and left his kingdom as a legacy to Rome (133 B.C.). Although in 88 B.C. there was a rebellion against Roman rule, this was suppressed by Sulla. By the time Paul arrived at Ephesus, it was a thoroughly Roman city in its government, and mostly Greek in its culture. It was also the most important city in the province of Asia.

The ruins of Ephesus are among the most thoroughly studied and most often visited in Asia Minor.

The Temple of Diana

You may (or some members of your class may) have referred to the great temple in Ephesus as the temple of Diana, rather than of Artemis. You may also have come across some translations where the rioters shouted "Great is Diana of the Ephesians!"

The reason for this is that from a very early date the Greek goddess Artemis became identified with the Roman Diana. It is not quite true to say that Diana and Artemis were two names for the same goddess. What actually happened was that (as the interaction between Romans and Greeks increased) there was an interest on both sides to find points of agreement or connection. Gods and goddesses with similar characteristics or functions tended to be equated with one another, even though originally they were quite distinct. Thus, a number of equivalences were created, such as Poseidon/Neptune; Aphrodite/Venus; Ares/Mars; and (what most interests us here) Artemis/Diana.

When the Book of Acts was translated from its original Greek into Latin, it was natural for Latin-speakers to translate "Artemis" as "Diana." This, in turn, gave rise to a long tradition in the West, so that even when translations were made into other Western languages, it was most common to say "Diana" instead of "Artemis."

Priscilla and Aquila

Were Priscilla and Aquila still in Ephesus during these events? It is impossible to tell. Their names are not mentioned. In fact, there is no mention of them during this entire second sojourn of Paul in Ephesus. In Romans 16:3-4 Paul says that "they risked their necks for my life." Some interpreters suggest that this occurred on the occasion of the riot in Ephesus. But in truth there is no way to either confirm or deny such a theory.

Gaius and Aristarchus

This is the first time that Aristarchus is mentioned in Acts. He apparently was a collaborator with Paul in various circumstances, for he appears again in Acts 20:4 and 27:2—in both cases, accompanying Paul on part of his journey. Paul himself mentions him in Colossians 4:10 and Philemon 24, sending greetings by him to those who would read his letters.

The case of Gaius presents more difficulties. He is mentioned again in Acts 20:4, together with Aristarchus. But there we are told that he was from Derbe—which is not in Macedonia. It is not clear whether this reference is to another person with the same name, and Luke told us that he was from Derbe in order to distinguish him from the other Gaius; or if for some other reason it could be said first that he was from Macedonia, and later that he was from Derbe—much as it may be said that the writer of this guide is from Cuba (having been born there) and also from Georgia (current residence). To complicate matters, Paul mentioned a Gaius who was with him in his greetings in Romans 16:23; and he also said that in Corinth he baptized Gaius (1 Corinthians 1:14). Since this was a very common name in the Roman Empire, in this list of references there are probably several persons with the same name; it is impossible to know how many.

Asiarchs

The term in verse 31 which the NRSV translates as "officials of the province of Asia" (and King James as "chiefs of Asia" is literally *Asiarchs*. There was in the region of Asia (part of what today is the tip of Turkey) a league of cities. This league was both a civil federation and a religious coalition and was represented by a person who had both priestly and civil functions. Thus, these "Asiarchs" were indeed officials of Asia; but they were not Roman officials. Rather, they were representatives of ancient traditions such as the one that in Ephesus had developed on the basis of the ancient Great Mother, and had eventually developed into the worship of Artemis.

It is difficult to imagine why these people would have befriended Paul. It is easier to imagine that, like the town clerk in Ephesus, they feared that if a Roman citizen such as Paul were hurt, this might bring undesirable consequences for them and their own cities and traditions.

12

Acts 23:23– 24:27

TRIAL

Opening Prayer

Kindle in us the fire of your love,
and strengthen our lives for service in your kingdom;
through your Son, Jesus Christ our Lord,
who lives and reigns with you in the unity of the Holy
    Spirit,
one God, now and forever. Amen.

(From *Book of Common Worship.* ©1993 Westminster/John Knox Press)

Dimension 1:
What Does the Bible Say?

(A) Tell the story.

There is a gap in the narrative between last week's text and the passage studied today. Begin the session by asking students to "fill in the gap."

- Ask:
—Where was Paul as we ended the session last week?
- With the help of the map, quickly track Paul's journey. Follow him to Macedonia and Greece, past Troas, and back to Miletus, near Ephesus, where he met with the elders from Ephesus. (This itinerary is in Acts 20.)
- Follow Paul back to Jerusalem, where he was arrested and nearly beaten.
- End with the plot to kill him, his learning of the plot, and his letting Claudius Lysias know.
- As locations are mentioned, use the length of ribbon or yarn from previous mappings and "tack" or staple it to the pertinent cities or other locations.

Teaching Tip

Since the class will have read all of this Scripture in their Daily Bible Journey, all you may have to do is jog their memories. Encourage students to verbalize the journey, mentioning the various places involved in Paul's travels and telling what they remember. Do not linger on details if students cannot remember; fill in the gaps left by students.

Optional Method

● A briefer option begins by asking the questions:
—Where was Paul when the action began in this story?
—How did he get there?

● In this case, rather than reviewing Paul's travels since Ephesus, all that is necessary is to say that he was in Jerusalem. Explain the events that led to his imprisonment.

(B) Review questions in the study book.

● If students have not answered the questions in the study book, page 93, give them an opportunity to do so now. Answers to the questions are as follows:

1. The story began in Jerusalem and ended in Caesarea.

2. The attitude varied. However, 24:5-6 probably summarizes the overall feelings of the authorities. Paul was a pest!

3. The Jewish leaders were adamantly opposed to Paul. Note 23:20-22.

4. Paul appeared before Felix—and, by the end of our passage, languished in prison for two years (24:27).

Dimension 2:
What Does the Bible Mean?

(C) Ask "why" questions.

● An excellent way to get people involved with this passage and studying it carefully involves asking a series of "why" questions:

—Why do you think that Claudius Lysias sent Paul to Felix in Caesarea? (There was a plot to kill Paul, and Lysias wished to avoid being tainted with the death of a Roman citizen under his custody. It was a sticky situation, with the Jewish leaders demanding that Lysias take a certain course of action; this was made difficult by Paul's Roman citizenship.)

—Why do you think Lysias detached such a large escort to accompany Paul? (Probably because he was afraid that the original plot could easily be revised, and they could have Paul killed under cover of some riot or disorder.)

—Why were they to leave at night? (Probably for similar reasons—so that those who were plotting Paul's death would be caught off balance, and it would take them some time to reorganize their plans.)

—Why did Lysias send a letter to Felix? (It was required by Roman legal procedures. It gave him an opportunity to explain and justify his actions before the governor.)

—Why did he say that he saved Paul's life because he was a Roman citizen, when the truth was that Paul was in fact already his prisoner when he learned that he was a Roman citizen? (Perhaps to paint himself in a better light before the governor.)

—Why did the infantry return to their barracks in Jerusalem once they had delivered Paul to Antipatris? (The heavier escort was no longer needed, since they were now far from Jerusalem, where the plot against Paul had been hatched. By continuing only with cavalry, Paul's escort would be able to move faster and arrive at Caesarea more quickly.)

—Why did the high priest Ananias come to Caesarea in person? (Probably because he considered the case to be of great importance. Perhaps because he bore a personal grudge against Paul, who had said some very harsh words to him before the Council; also because Paul had very adroitly divided the Council by calling himself a Pharisee and turning the debate toward the question of the resurrection of the dead—see Acts 23:2-10.)

—Why did he bring Tertullus with him? (He wanted the case to be presented in the best possible manner, following all the Roman legal forms, in order to make certain that Paul would be found guilty.)

—Why did Tertullus open his speech with so much flattery towards Felix? (Because that was the custom at the time, when speeches were expected to begin with an attempt to gain the good will of the addressees. Because he did not care whether he told the truth or not, as long as he got a conviction.)

—Why did Paul begin his speech with such scant words about Felix? (Because there was little that he could say about Felix that was good, and he was not willing to bend the truth in order to be acquitted.)

—Why did Tertullus call Paul a "pestilent fellow, an agitator," a "ringleader" who tried to profane the Temple? (Because, as an accuser, he had to present Paul in the worst possible light. Because he knew that at least the accusations of being an agitator, and of seeking to profane the Temple, would call the attention of Roman authorities, and especially of the Roman governor of the province.)

—Why did Paul deny that he was an agitator, and that he had tried to profane the Temple, but readily accepted the accusation of Tertullus that he was" a ringleader of the sect of the Nazarenes"? (Because being an agitator or profaning the Temple would have been real crimes, punishable by Roman law, and on which the governor would have to take action. The accusation of being a Christian leader was, first of all, true; and, second, not a crime that a Roman governor would be interested in punishing.)

—Why do you think that Felix adjourned the meeting, and left his decision pending? (Because if he decided in favor of Paul he would alienate these Jewish leaders, whom he still had to govern; and if he decided in favor of Paul's accusers, his decision would probably be overturned by a higher court, thus putting him in a bad light. Because he was hoping that Paul, who apparently had enough resources to have brought alms to Jerusalem (Acts 24:17), would be willing to pay a bribe for his freedom.)

—Why do you think that Felix ordered that Paul be kept in custody, but with relatively lenient conditions? (It was obvious that Paul was not a dangerous criminal. If his friends could come and take care of his needs, he would later have no reason to complain about the treatment he had received, even if he were eventually acquitted. Thus, by keeping Paul in prison, Felix kept Ananias and his party content; and by allowing him "some liberty" he avoided a possible complaint on Paul's part later on.)

—Why do you think that Felix decided to have another interview with Paul while Drusilla was present? (Perhaps because, since Drusilla was Jewish, she might help him understand some of the issues that were at stake. Perhaps because this might be a form of amusement.)

—Why do you think that Felix was frightened when he heard Paul speak of "justice, self-control, and the coming judgment"? (We know from other historical documents that Felix was not a just governor, and that one thing he clearly lacked was self-control. Paul was speaking about how these were necessary, and how those who did not practice justice and self-control would have to face God's coming judgment.)

—Why do you think that Felix allowed two years to pass while Paul continued to be confined in prison, and eventually ended his own governorship leaving the matter pending? (Because this was a situation in which, no matter what verdict he rendered, there was nothing to gain and much to lose. Better leave it for someone else to handle.)

Teaching Tip

Obviously, this method could occupy your entire session. Maximize involvement by dividing your class membership into smaller discussion groups of three to five persons. Assign to each group certain questions rather than all of them. Allow ample time for research and discussion. Provide a resource table on which students can discover commentaries, Bibles of several translations, and other study helps from your church or public library or pastor's study. Invite each discussion group to report highlights of their discussion when the class meets in a large group context.

(D) Identify the main characters in the passage.

As on previous occasions, this text could also be illumined by simply making a "cast of characters."

- Using chalkboard and chalk or markers and newsprint, list the main actors in the story. You will end with a list that will look more or less as follows: Paul, Claudius Lysias, Felix, Ananias Tertullus, Drusilla, (Porcius Festus—who appears between parentheses because only in the next chapter will we be told more about his actions).

- When the list is completed, ask class members to share what each character did and, as far as possible, why. (You may wish to leave Paul for last, since so much more is known about him, and in any case talking about his actions and motivations would be a good bridge into Dimension 3.)

- As the participants talk, record two or three words next to each name on your list as a summary of what they did and why.

- By the time you have finished this process, the class will have examined the text quite thoroughly and probably will have come up with some significant insights into the text itself.

Dimension 3: What Does the Bible Mean to Us?

(E) Appraise Paul's integrity.

The study book describes Paul's integrity when facing Felix.

- Share in a mini-lecture:

> Paul's very life may have depended on the impression he made on the Roman governor. Yet, in contrast to Tertullus, Paul did not flatter Felix. He was respectful but truthful. He could not say much good about Felix's governorship; he remained silent about it and simply noted the fact that "for many years you have been a judge over this nation" (10). The point is that we should take this as an example of the integrity to be expected of Christians.
>
> In our society, we are seldom confronted with people who have such power of life and death over us. We are often confronted with people who, at an infinitely lower level, give us an opportunity to practice Christian integrity.

- In order to provoke a discussion on this subject, ask the class to imagine the following situation:
  You are members of a visiting team from the church, going out to see members in order to ask their pledges for the church's budget. You go to the house of one of the wealthiest members of the church. He is polite, invites you to come in and sit down, and then proceeds to tell you how he feels about the church: "The church," he says, "would do much better if it would just quit dabbling in all kinds of issues in which it has no business. Last

year they began agitating for that half-way house for ex-convicts that the city put here in our neighborhood. Let me tell you something, with what I lost in the value of this property alone I could have kept the church going for a whole year! Now they have all those people with AIDS coming to church. Do they expect my daughter to sit right there next to them? I tell you, the church better get its act together and quit rocking the boat, or it will sink, boat and all! You give your pastor my pledge. But make sure you tell her that!"

● Ask the class:

—What would you do in such a situation?

● Consider, as part of your conversation these options:

—You thank the man, pray with him, and leave as quickly as possible.

—You tell him that you are sure the church will appreciate his support, but that he should not expect it to change its stance just because he is such a large donor and is so upset.

—You try to show him that the gospel requires that the church do these things that he so dislikes.

—You tell him to keep his pledge, and to give it directly to the pastor, when he can tell her how he feels.

—You show sympathy, tell him that your property values have also gone down, lead him to understand that you see things the same way he does, when in fact you do not.

● Discuss these and other options mentioned by participants.

● After some discussion, focus again on the text. Ask:

—How are our various answers similar to Paul's attitude before Felix?

—How are they different?

Optional Method

Set up the same item for reflection; but instead of just having a discussion, have it presented as a roleplay.

● Invite two participants to play the role of the visiting team, and another participant, the role of the wealthy host.

● Those roleplaying the situation should portray the visit with the man, spontaneously responding to his objections to the church's various ministries.

● If you wish, you could have several "visiting teams" try their hand at dealing with this "prospective donor." Give each no more than two or three minutes to try their hand at it.

● After the roleplay, lead the class in a discussion of the issues involved, especially the issue of integrity when speaking with those with whom we disagree.

(F) Consider how the story helps you face difficulties.

One of the themes brought up in the study book is Paul's patience and endurance in a difficult situation. Remember that at the beginning of our study we said that one of Luke's

concerns in writing Acts was the very real possibility that Christians might suffer duress and even persecution, and preparing them for such an eventuality.

● Ask the class:

—Do you think that the story of Paul's imprisonment and repeated trials would have strengthened Christians facing the possibility of persecution?

—Today we may not be threatened with persecution. Are there other situations in life in which this story can strengthen you and help you face difficulties?

(G) Explore your ability to cope.

It is clear that Paul had resources that helped him withstand the ordeal described in these final chapters of Acts.

● Ask the class:

—What inner resources do you think Paul had in order to be able to withstand such a difficult and seemingly endless situation? (As students respond, remember that Paul was allowed visits and help from his "friends," who would be other believers. Thus, he was not relying only on his inner resources, but also on the community of faith.)

—Do we have the same resources?

—How do we see them at work in our lives today?

—Is there any way we can prepare ourselves so that those resources will be there when we most desperately need them?

—Is it true, as Paul says in Romans, that "suffering produces endurance, and endurance produces character, and character produces hope"? (Romans 5:3-4)

—Have you ever experienced this condition in your own life?

—Have you seen it at work in the lives of others?

—What resources have sustained you in difficult times? Prayer? Bible reading and meditation? Hymns and singing? The support and understanding of others?

(H) Pray.

● End the session with a prayer:

God of all power and all creation, we thank you for your constant love and care. We pray that you will make us feel your presence so closely and so surely, that even in the most difficult of circumstances we will not despair. We pray also that, just as others have sustained us in times of difficulty, we too may sustain others when their times of trial come. In the name of Jesus, who underwent all trials for our sake. Amen.

Additional Bible Helps

Paul's Escorting Force
The force that Lysias ordered to escort Paul was impressive: a total of four hundred and seventy men. The two hundred

"soldiers" were infantry. The seventy were cavalry. It is not clear what the other two hundred were. The NRSV calls them **"spearmen,"** but the truth is that the name that they were given in the original is sufficiently uncommon that translators are not certain what it means. They could also be bowmen, or another auxiliary unit of light cavalry. Later, when in verses 31 and 32 the forces divide with the infantry returning and the cavalry continuing to Caesarea, it is not clear whether these other 200 "spearmen" were among those who returned or among those who continued.

Felix

We know of Felix from Roman historians Tacitus and Suetonius, as well as from the Jewish writer Flavius Josephus. None of these historians painted a very positive picture of him. He was a freedman who had moved up in the world through the patronage of Agrippina, Nero's mother. In order to advance his career, he married three influential women—which is the reason why Suetonius mockingly called him "husband of three queens." Tacitus, on his part, depicted him as a man given to licentiousness and cruelty, a tyrant who "ruled as if he were a king, but with the spirit of a slave." He was appointed governor of Judea towards the end of Claudius' reign. Since Claudius died in A.D. 54, Felix must have already been governor of Judea for some four years when Paul was brought before him (probably A.D. 58).

The picture that Luke drew of him in Acts 24:25, as a man who became frightened when he heard of "justice, self-control, and the coming judgment," is perfectly compatible with what we know of him through these other sources.

The Charge of Agitation

When Tertullus accused Paul of being an "agitator," the Greek word that was used is the same word that the town clerk in Ephesus employed when he suggested that if the riot continued, the entire city could be accused of sedition. Remember the reaction in Ephesus when the possibility of such an accusation came up. Thus, the charge that Tertullus brought against Paul was serious.

Roman Laws Regarding Custody

There were basically three ways in which a prisoner could be kept in custody under Roman law. The harshest was **public custody** in which the prisoner was kept in jail and chained. (See Acts 12:6, where Peter was guarded in an extreme form of this sort of custody, with a guard chained to each arm.) The second was **military custody** in which a prisoner was chained to a soldier when being transported or under other special circumstances, but which allowed for the removal of chains when the person was in an enclosure. Under some circumstances, people could visit such a prisoner, and even bring meals or render other similar services. Finally, there was **free custody** which was similar to "house arrest." Apparently what Felix ordered was a mild form of the second type of custody. Later, in Rome, Paul's situation became more like a "free custody" or house arrest.

Drusilla

Drusilla was one of the "three queens" whom Felix married in his ascent to power. She was a younger daughter of King Herod Agrippa I, who had ordered the death of James (see Acts 12) and the imprisonment of Peter. Therefore, she was also a sister of Herod Agrippa II and Bernice, who would later also have the opportunity to hear Paul (see Acts 25:13–26:36).

Before marrying Felix, Drusilla had been the wife of King Aziz of Emesa, but she had left him in order to marry Felix. We know of at least one son of hers, Agrippa, who died with her when Vesuvius erupted in A.D. 79.

Preventative Custody

The reference to "two years" in verse 27 is significant. According to Roman law, two years was the maximum amount of time a prisoner could be kept under preventive custody. At the end of that time, he must either have been condemned and punished, or let go. In this case, however, Felix simply let that time lapse, according to Luke, in order to "grant the Jews a favor" (24:27). He may have been still hoping to receive a bribe. Also, one may imagine that once he had learned of the coming of a new governor he would much rather have left the problem for his successor than deal with it himself.

One of Luke's concerns was the attitude of the Roman authorities towards Christianity. He showed that when Roman officials treated Christians harshly they did so for their own reasons, and not as good, faithful representatives of Rome and its laws.

Porcius Festus

It is difficult to determine the exact date at which Porcius Festus succeeded Felix as governor, but the most likely date is the year A.D. 60. Thus, Paul would have been arrested in Jerusalem at some point in A.D. 58, then taken to Caesarea, and remained there, in a sort of legal limbo, until the year A.D. 60.

Little is known of Porcius Festus himself. Jewish historian Flavius Josephus describes him as an energetic and efficient person. Once again, this coincides with what Luke recorded about his actions in the very next chapter, where Festus followed a policy that was diametrically opposed to the delays of Felix.

13

Acts 27:1– 28:10

SHIPWRECK

Opening Prayer

Come, Holy Spirit!
Rain upon our dry and dusty lives.
Wash away our sin
and heal our wounded spirits.
Kindle within us the fire of your love
to burn away our apathy.
With your warmth bend our rigidity,
and guide our wandering feet. Amen.

(From *Book of Common Worship.* ©1993 Westminster/John Knox Press)

Dimension 1:
What Does the Bible Say?

As students arrive, encourage them to note significant learnings from their studies during the previous twelve sessions. Provide them with large sheets of newsprint and markers or chalkboard and chalk. "Prime the pump" by noting one or two of your most significant learnings using the materials provided before students arrive.

(A) Map Paul's journey.

- Throughout your study on Paul you have identified significant stops on Paul's journey. Finish tracking the journey. Use the map, tacks or staples, and length of yarn or string from earlier sessions.
- In this session the following "stops" should be noted on the map: The trip to Rome began (in chapter 27) at Sidon, continued across the sea off Cilicia and Pamphylia to Myra in Lycia. After difficulties, the ship arrived near Cnidus, sailing near the island of Crete off Salmone to Fair Havens, near Lasea. By verse 16, the ship was near an island called Cauda and, by verse 27, the ship was drifting across the sea of Adria. Chapter 28 records that the group had reached safety on the island of Malta. After a resting time of three months, the ship put in at Syracuse and then, after three days, came to Rhegium, Puteoli, and finally to Rome. Paul lived in Rome for two years.

(B) Review the the passage.

The passage studied in this session is lengthy. It is also among the most interesting! Rather than read the passage, involve participants in storytelling.

- Begin the story: "It was decided to set sail for Italy. Paul, other prisoners, Aristarchus, a centurion named Julius, and other people traveled by ship."
- Use the map from activity (A) to remember the various stops in Paul's travels.
- Encourage participants to remember details of the story (debates regarding the safest route, the throwing of wheat into the sea, and so forth). Do not become overly concerned about remembering every detail.
- As one participant adds a detail to the story, another may continue the story.

Teaching Tip

To keep the story moving and the climate of the session lighthearted, toss a ball from storyteller to storyteller. As long as the ball is held in the hands of one participant, he or she tells the story. When the ball is tossed to another person, that participant becomes the storyteller.

(C) Review the questions in the study book.

- The answers to Dimension 1 questions can be discovered by reading Acts 27:1–28:10.
- Review the questions and the answers of students.

The answers to the Dimension 1 questions are not simple.

1. Where did Paul sail from? Who was with him? (Paul sailed twice. The first leg of the journey in one ship took him to Myra in Lycia. The second leg, in a larger ship, ended in shipwreck on Malta. The companions whom Luke mentioned at the beginning presumably continued with Paul on the second leg—persons such as the centurion, his soldiers, and Aristarchus. Thus, not all the 276 people who were on board when the shipwreck took place, sailed with Paul from Caesarea.)

2. What was Paul's position in the ship? Did this change as the story developed? Did his authority increase or wane? Why? (The name of Aristarchus as one of Paul's companions, but not as a prisoner, as well as the narrator who used the "we" form, indicated that apparently the conditions of Paul's imprisonment were the same, for he was allowed, as Felix had decided, to have friends travel with him to take care of his needs.)

Teaching Tip

The question of who sailed with Paul will most likely lead someone to ask, "Who is telling the story and telling it now in the first person singular?" Once someone poses this question, you may wish to move to activity (D) in Dimension 2.

(D) Consider who told the story.

The problems raised by the "we" sections (see Additional Bible Helps, page 67, of this leader's guide) may be turned from problems into a significant insight as to the purpose of the entire Book of Acts.

- When someone raises the question of who it is that constitutes the "we" (in other words, who the narrator is) give the references to the other "we" sections in Acts.
- Call the attention of the class to the diagram called "The Weave of Acts," page 111. The diagram shows that characters come in and out of the story at various points. Seldom does Acts tell us why a character is no longer in the picture. Underscore this by showing that the same is true of a number of other characters. (Toward the end of the session, you may also point out that, although the last chapters of Acts deal primarily with Paul, the book ends without telling us what happened to him in the end.) Explain that the reason for this is not that Luke was a disjointed, or disorganized narrator. The reason is rather that Luke's main character is neither Paul, nor any of the apostles, but the Holy Spirit.

  The very scheme of having people come in and out of the scene is a way of showing that, after all, none of these people is the center of the story. The book is not about the apostles. It is not about Paul. It is not about the adventures of the author while on shipboard with Paul. **It is about the Holy Spirit, who guides and strengthens all of these other secondary characters.** Precisely by not following any of these characters as if the book were a biography, Acts centers the reader's attention on the Spirit and the Spirit's actions.

(E) Invite a sailing enthusiast to speak.

- If you have a sailing enthusiast in your class, ask this person to study the passage beforehand, then to explain to the class what is happening. This passage is full of details of sailing and the handling of ships under sail.
- Students interested in researching details regarding this sailing trip will benefit by using Bible commentaries and different translations of the passage.

(F) Examine the dynamics between Paul and the centurion.

- Prior to the session, invite two students to roleplay the roles of Paul and the centurion as part of the class session. There are several stages in this relationship.
—When they arrived at Sidon, the centurion treated Paul

"kindly," and allowed him to go visit his "friends." (Do not forget that, when on shore, Paul was most likely chained by the arm to a Roman soldier.)

—In Fair Havens, Paul offered his advice to the effect that they should remain there for the winter. The centurion paid more attention to the pilot and the owner and decided not to heed Paul's warning.

—At sea, in the middle of the storm, Paul spoke words of encouragement to all on board. He reminded them that he had warned them before, as a way to give more strength to his promise that they would be spared.

—Once close to shore, and after the ship was anchored from the stern, Paul persuaded the soldiers (and presumably their leader, the centurion) to cut the ship's boat adrift, so that the sailors could not escape on it.

—Just before daybreak, Paul spoke further words of encouragement and signaled his own hope by eating. The others, encouraged by his example, also ate.

—As the ship was breaking up, the soldiers were considering the possibility of killing the prisoners so that they might not escape. But the centurion, in order to save Paul, gave the order that all were to be given a chance to make it to the shore.

Optional Method

- Invite the same two people to play their roles, as in activity (F), but ask the other class members to imagine that they are the soldiers, sailors, and other prisoners and passengers.
- Post an outline of the relationship development between Paul and the centurion on a chalkboard or newsprint.
- Encourage students to think about their reactions at each point in the narrative.
- If they wish, students can break into the roleplay, always playing the role of one of these other people on board and trying to express their attitudes and reactions.

Dimension 3:
What Does the Bible Mean to Us?

(G) Consider Paul's expertise.

Dimension 3 of the study book indicates that there are times when Christians speak, not necessarily out of technical expertise, but rather out of a combination of common sense and vision. This kind of speaking is similar to what Paul employed when he warned his companions not to sail out of Fair Havens. The study book underscores the fact that some-

times the "experts," although they know all the technical details, lack the vision (or the commitment) to give fair and true warning of the storms of life. (Examples given pertain to ecological and economic issues.)

- Ask the class:
—Why do you think Paul was able to warn the people on board that it was dangerous to sail at that time? (As we read the text in 27:10, it appears that he had a vision or some other such indication, for he says "I can see that the voyage will be with danger and much heavy loss." It also appears that Paul employed common sense (Share information about Paul's common sense, as provided in the Additional Bible Helps section, page 66, of this leader's guide.)
—Why do you think that the pilot and the owner of the ship, who must have been experts on sea travel, could not see the reason for what Paul said? (A possible answer is that they were interested in moving on to get as close to Rome as possible, so that early in the next season their ship would be one of the very first in, thus being able to sell their cargo at a premium.)

- Share:
As you know, for a long time there have been strong elements in the churches that were campaigning against the use of tobacco. Many of us felt that this was a misguided campaign, based on moralistic considerations on the part of people who were intent on running other people's lives. Recent information indicates that tobacco is addictive and quite harmful, both to the smoker and to those affected by the secondhand smoke.
—Given some of the recent studies regarding tobacco use, how do you think a Christian should respond?
—Did the church, out of common sense and a vision of the purpose of human life, have a vision that the experts did not have or could not express?

Optional Method

- Choose a subject that is being debated in the newspapers as you prepare this class.
- Learn what the "experts" say on both sides of the issue. (Even better, get some members of the class to learn what these experts are saying.)
- Bring a report to the class (or have the members who studied the matter make that report.) **Make certain that it is a balanced report in which the experts on both sides get equal time, and their arguments are presented with equal care and seriousness.**
- Having shown that the experts can support both sides, ask:
—On what bases should Christians come to a decision regarding this matter?

Optional Method

Turn to the second point made in the study book, namely, that an obedient church is a boon to the society around it, and a disobedient church may be a threat to it. Ask:

—Do you think this is true?
—Can you think of other instances where the faithfulness of a few might have saved the many? (Think, for instance, of the story of Sodom, which God would have spared had there been ten righteous in it (Genesis 18:16-32).

(H) Discuss the importance of Acts 27:33-38.

● Read aloud Acts 27:33-38. This is that part of the story where, just before the final shipwreck, Paul took bread, gave thanks, broke it, and ate.
● Note that there was some debate among Bible interpreters as to whether this was a Communion celebration or not. In any case, the allusion is clearly intended, for the four verbs employed, and in that order, are the same that appear in most ancient descriptions of the Lord's Supper: *took bread*, *gave thanks*, *broke it*, and *ate*. It thus appears that Paul may have celebrated the very center of Christian worship on deck in the presence of these non-believers.
● Ask the class:
—Do you see any connection between this passage and what Paul said in 1 Corinthians, that every time we eat this bread and drink of this cup, we announce the death of the Lord?
—In other words, is there a sense in which Christian wor-

ship, whether public or private, reminds the world (even the unbelieving world) of a Lord whom it so often and so easily forgets?
—Do you think that the church today, like Paul on that ship, gives assurance to the world?
● Share:
In today's world there is as much despair as there must have been on that ship. People are worried about their own survival, and they are also worried about the survival of the earth and of the human species. In our cities, and increasingly in smaller towns, people live in fear of crime. Many have given up, and live for the pleasure of the moment, often prisoners of addictions that bring even more despair.
● In that context, ask the class:
—How can the church be a sign of hope, as Paul was a sign of hope to the people on that ship?
—Do you believe that people who today are despairing of the future would see our worship as a sign of hope?

(I) Discuss the article "Acts 29?"

● Look at the section in the study book called "Acts 29?"
● In essence, the article suggests that the Book of Acts does not end, precisely as a sign that the "acts of the Spirit," which is its main theme, had not ended. The book is not about the apostles or about Paul. It is about the Spirit. In that sense, we are still living in what that section calls "Acts 29."
● Ask the class if they have read that section. If not, either summarize it or give students an opportunity to read it.
● Ask:
—Where do you see the Spirit at work today?

(J) Write a new ending.

● Drawing upon some of the material from the article in the study book entitled "Acts 29?", invite participants to "write" an "extra chapter" to Acts, telling a story of how they have seen the Spirit active in their own lives, or in the lives of those around them.
● Divide the class into teams of three to five members and give them the task of discussing what should be included in such a chapter.
● Allow teams approximately seven minutes to work. When time has elapsed, bring everyone back together in the large-class format.
● Invite a member of each writing team to share what they think should be included.

(K) Plan a "farewell" celebration.

● Since this session is the last of this particular volume of JOURNEY THROUGH THE BIBLE, plan a final gathering at some other time. Perhaps a shared meal or a dessert potluck would be celebration options.

- If you hold a farewell celebration, and if you used learning activity (J), save the chapters and read them as part of the farewell celebration.

(L) End the session in prayer.

We thank you, God, for your servant Luke, who has so blessed us with the books he wrote. We thank you for our class and all that we have learned from each other and from you. We thank you for your Spirit, who has been at work in the church through the ages and still works within us. We pray that, by your Spirit, we may prove worthy heirs of the story we have studied, and witnesses to your truth and grace. We pray in the name of Jesus, your Son and our Lord. Amen.

Additional Bible Helps

The "We" Passages

You will note that in this passage the story is told in the first person plural ("we"). Most of the Book of Acts is written in the third person ("he", "they"). There are some sections, especially toward the end, which are in the first person, as if the author had been part of the events.

Scholars have debated about these sections (usually called the "we passages"), and have not come to a universally accepted explanation. Some claim that at this point Luke was making use of a travelogue written by someone who had accompanied Paul. Others suggest that it was just a general sea narrative, which Luke then interpolated in order to bring Paul into it. Still others propose the theory that the "we" is a rhetorical or a theological clue, suggesting for instance that a certain passage is particularly important. Most of these explanations seem far-fetched.

There is no real reason to reject the obvious explanation: that the author of Acts (the same one who also wrote the Gospel of Luke) was with Paul during these events, and therefore simply did what anyone would do under such circumstances—switch to the first person plural. If "Theophilus" was an actual individual, he may even have known that the author of Luke/Acts had been part of this story and would not have found the "we" sections at all surprising.

One difficulty is that if you read the story in Acts, trying to follow when the "we" joined Paul and when it left him, there is no continuity. At some points, the "we" disappear with no logical reason, only to reappear later, again with no explanation. (Try this if you like: the "we" passages—apart from one other place in which various manuscripts do not agree—are 16:10-17; 20:5-15; 21:5-18; and 27:1–28:16. You will soon discover that the "we" comes on board, so to speak, with no announcement or explanation, and disappears in the same manner.)

This, however, should not surprise us, for that is the practice of the entire Book of Acts with all its characters. Not only the "we," but also Silas, Timothy, and even Peter, seem to come suddenly into the story, and then to disappear just as suddenly.

Fair Havens

The city of Lasea in Crete is now in ruins. Near it there is a small port called Kololomonias. This may be a corruption of its ancient Greek name that Acts gives as *Kalous limenas*—Fair Havens.

The Fast

The reference to "the Fast" in verse 9 requires some explanation. The Fast to which reference is made was the Jewish celebration of *Kippur,* on the tenth day of the month of Tishri. The time in the solar year when this fell varied from year to year, but it usually took place in late September or early October. It was a quick way of determining the sailing season, for normally after "the Fast," the winter storms of the eastern Mediterranean posed a growing danger. It was customary for ships to remain at anchor, or at least not to attempt long voyages, until the spring.

In the year A.D. 59, which is the probable date of the events that Luke was narrating, Kippur fell on October 5—almost as late as was possible. Therefore, if "the Fast" had already gone by, it must have been mid-October—a dangerous time to sail the eastern Mediterranean. Thus, Paul's warnings are not entirely based on religious insight or inspiration; he is also making use of common sense and of the sailing tradition and lore that all sailors used.

POWER GIVEN ME TO TEACH

by Bradford Motta

Most of us have read or heard the story about the Day of Pentecost as told in the second chapter of Acts. The disciples were gathered together when suddenly a sound from the heavens filled the meeting place and was heard by people in the city. People ran to the house to see what was happening, and what they found amazed them.

They stood, listening to the disciples speak, and to their amazement they all could understand. The Parthians understood what was being said. The Elamites understood. Others who spoke other languages were able to understand the Galilean men. The power of the Spirit had changed them. Even though they spoke different languages, they were able to understand the words of the disciples.

The people were overjoyed. The Spirit of God was upon them, and they were overwhelmed by its power and presence. The mood was so different, the spirits so high, the emotions so celebrative, that some people discounted the event by claiming that the people were drunk. At that point in the story Peter stood up and reminded the people of the words of the prophet Joel:

I will pour out my spirit upon all flesh,
    and your sons and your daughters shall prophesy,
and your young men shall see visions,
    and your old men shall dream dreams.

(Acts 2:17).

The Day of Pentecost was not just a nice experience. At Pentecost came a power to be reckoned with. People felt different. People acted different. And Peter proclaimed that this was just the beginning.

As Sunday school teachers, we teach the stories of the faith. Sometimes the details of a story are difficult to get across; but with the help of timelines, maps, and a few commentaries, we are able to make them clear. Even the story of Pentecost can be told with attention to detailing the events. Who was there? What actually happened? What did Peter say? What did the people do? These questions point to facts.

But the story of Pentecost is more than facts about an incident. This story declares God's power in the world. When we teach, we can focus on the facts of the story, or we can declare the power.

Declaring the Power

We declare the power of God by using it. Our active faith is a declaration. Every time we open ourselves to God's presence and ask for God's guidance, we are declaring that God does have power in our lives.

The very act of prayer is a declaration of faith. We pray because we know God hears us and is with us. Declaring our faith may not require us to stand up and make some grand announcement; it may simply consist of opening class with a prayer.

Peter stood up before the people on the Day of Pentecost and declared that God's Spirit was on the loose and that people would begin to have visions, dream dreams, and prophesy. As teachers, how do we claim that power?

Claiming the Power

Each week, we as teachers are faced with preparing for the next week's lesson. For some, preparation means opening a teacher book to a lesson plan and making plans. For others, it requires in-depth Bible study and careful note taking.

Whichever situation you are in, do you begin your preparation by calling on God for understanding and guidance? That's the first step to claiming the power. The presence of God in our teaching is revealed through our attitude toward God. When we invite God into the everyday events of our lives, we claim God's power. It is so easy for us to get busy with the lesson plan, to get all the facts down about God's presence in the world and yet forget to call on God.

Peter reminded the people, using Joel's words, that the Spirit has tremendous power for our lives. As teachers we need to recognize that God is with us in our teaching ministry and that God will do wondrous things if we just invite God in.

Questions for Reflection

1. Before you plan your next lesson, take a moment for silent meditation. Ask God to be present with you. Thank God for your class and the challenges it presents. Ask God to give you insights into the Scripture passage for the lesson. Consider this time well spent; it is just as important as the time you spend reading the lesson material. Allow God to prepare the soil for planting.

2. Identify times when you have felt the active presence of God's Spirit in your life. How has God been present in your life? How has God's presence given you strength and power for living? Seek opportunities to share those experiences with the class.

3. Provide opportunities for your class to talk about the presence of God in their lives. There is always time for giving opinions or interpretations of Scripture. Provide time for people to interpret how God is working in their lives.

Prayer

O God, thank you for your presence in my life and for the power of your Spirit. Help me be willing to open my life to your power. I get so busy, even when I am doing your work, that I forget to call on you. Be present in my teaching and learning so that through me people will see you. I pray this in the name of Jesus Christ my Lord. Amen.

Brad Motta, a former editor of Teacher, *is currently pastor of The United Methodist Church of Pearl River in Pearl River, New York.*

From Teacher in the Church Today, *May 1989, pages 22-23. Copyright © 1989 by Graded Press.*

GENTILES

by Cheryl Reames

Have you ever read a book and had a hard time figuring where a group of people fit in? Maybe on one page you thought, "These people are the bad guys." But on another page you suspected, "At the end these people will be the good guys." But then you thought, "These are not the major people in the story. By the end of the book will they still have a part in the story?" At times as you have read various passages in the Bible, you might have wondered these things about the Gentiles.

In the Bible the word for *Gentiles* is translated in various ways. In some places in the Bible *Gentiles* is translated as "heathen" and "pagans." In both the Old and New Testaments, the word *Gentiles* is often translated as "nations." The word *Gentiles* is used when the word signifies the non-Jewish nations in contrast to the Jews. But the word *nations* does not always refer to Gentiles. Sometimes it can mean all nations, including Jews.

In the drama of the Bible there are three main actors: God, the nations, and Israel (the Jewish nation).

Division Into Jews and Gentiles

According to Genesis, after the flood Noah's descendants divided into families that developed into nations and spread across the earth. When some of these descendants decided to build a tower to heaven to make a name for themselves, God became angry, confused their languages so that they could not understand one another, and scattered the peoples over all the earth (Genesis 11:1-9).

These stories of the beginnings of the earth's nations set the context for God's call to Abraham (Genesis 12:1-3). In that call God promised Abraham that his descendants would become a great nation and a blessing for all the families to the earth (Genesis 12:3). Israel as God's chosen people, set apart from the nations, would be born.

Observers, Tempters, Enemies

The Old Testament reflects several attitudes toward the Gentiles. Understanding themselves to be God's chosen people, the Jews interpreted God's actions primarily in terms of their own faithfulness or disobedience to the covenant established with Abraham and renewed through

Moses. In many cases the Gentiles were simply onlookers who feared God's power (Exodus 15:14) or who feared the Jews because of God's power (Deuteronomy 2:25).

At other times the Jews viewed the Gentiles as tempters. The Jews were called to be a holy nation and give their loyalty only to God. Yet the ways of the Gentiles—their fertility cults, occult arts, sacred kingship, and military power—were tempting and appealing to the Jews. The Jews feared the Gentiles would contaminate their religion and customs. There was always the possibility that the Jews might say, "Let us become like the nations, like the tribes of the countries, and worship wood and stone" (Ezekiel 20:32). Many Jewish laws prohibited contact between Jews and Gentiles to prevent religious and cultural contamination.

Gentiles were sometimes seen as enemies of the Jews and as enemies of God. From a political viewpoint, most of the Old Testament tells of Israel's struggles to remain an independent nation, free of foreign (Gentile) rule. As already mentioned, from a religious viewpoint Israel struggled to remain faithful to the one God, free of idolatry.

In Amos 1:3–2:4, an oracle tells of God's judgment on the Gentiles for their pride and violence. Some Bible passages talk of the Gentiles as the oppressors and plunderers of the Jews (Isaiah 41:11-12; 42:23-25). The Jews often viewed Gentiles as people who humiliated them. The prophet Jeremiah even asked God to "pour out your [God's] wrath on the nations that do not know you" (Jeremiah 10:25).

There was extreme animosity, bitterness, and hatred between Gentiles and Jews, so much so that the Jews cried to God for revenge. Yet there were still hints that the Gentiles would one day be blessed if they would turn to God.

The Gentiles as Israel's Mission

In Isaiah 49:6, God tells the Jews that they are to be a light to the Gentiles. And the Book of Zechariah tells of the messianic king who will bring blessings to all nations—Jews and Gentiles (Zechariah 9:9-10).

Ultimately, the Jewish people understood their role to be the means through which God would bless the Gentiles.

Their faith and life together were to point to the one true God in such a way that all the nations would be drawn to worship God and to enter into a covenant relationship with God.

Gentiles in the New Testament

According to the New Testament writers, the promise made to Abraham was fulfilled through Jesus. Matthew writes in his Gospel that Jesus came to fulfill what had been spoken by the prophet Isaiah: the servant would proclaim justice to the Gentiles and "in his name the Gentiles will hope" (Matthew 12:17-21).

At the presentation of the infant Jesus in the Temple, Simeon called him "a light for revelation to the Gentiles" (Luke 2:32). Jesus began his ministry in "Galilee of the Gentiles" (Matthew 4:15). The multitudes came to Jesus from beyond Jewish territory (Mark 3:8).

Although Jesus was a Jew, he was rather lax about contact with Gentiles. This earned him criticism by his enemies. Jesus ministered to several Gentiles: the Phoenician girl (Matthew 15:21-18; Mark 7:24-30), the Gerasene demoniac who then became a missionary to his own people (Mark 5:19-20), the servant of a Roman centurion (Matthew 8:5-13; Luke 7:1-10).

More than once Jesus sent his disciples on missions to the Gentiles (see Luke 10). Even Jesus' entry into Jerusalem revealed him to be the king who was to bring blessings of peace to the nations (Matthew 21:5).

Yet despite some sense of mission to the Gentiles and some willingness to deal with them, even Jesus used the Gentiles as an example of what God's people should not do. Jesus instructed his followers not to worry about what they would eat or drink, admonishing that "it is the Gentiles who strive for all these things" (Matthew 6:32).

Jesus also displayed some reluctance to deal with Gentiles. In Matthew 10:5 Jesus instructed his disciples to "go nowhere among the Gentiles and enter no town of the Samaritans." His disciples were to go to the lost sheep of Israel.

Jesus also pictured the Gentiles as those who would obstruct God. In foretelling his crucifixion and resurrection, he told that the religious authorities would hand the Son of Man "over to the Gentiles to be mocked and flogged and crucified" (Matthew 20:19). When Jesus foretold of the destruction of Jerusalem, he said that Jerusalem would "be trampled on by the Gentiles, until the times of the Gentiles are fulfilled" (Luke 21:24).

Changing Attitudes Toward Gentiles

After Jesus' resurrection, the apostle Peter, showing the traditional Jewish attitude, hesitated to associate with Gentiles. It took a vision from God to convince Peter to change his attitude toward Gentiles. Because of the vision, Peter realized that there was no longer any reason to refrain from associating with Gentiles.

When Peter preached to the Gentiles assembled at the home of Cornelius, the Holy Spirit was poured out on all the Gentiles who were listening. So Peter baptized the Gentile listeners (Acts 10:44-48).

When the apostles and other followers of Christ heard that Peter had baptized Gentiles who had accepted God's word, they were angry. Many believed that Gentiles had to be circumcised and obey Jewish law in order to become a follower of Jesus.

This issue continued to present problems as Paul began to travel throughout Asia Minor, establishing churches with many Gentile converts. The inclusion of Gentiles within the infant Christian community forced the New Testament Christians to reflect on what basis God established a relationship with God's people.

A Right Relationship With God

At the heart of the controversy was the question, How can a person have a right relationship with God? Paul said that living by Jewish law could not bring people into that relationship (Galatians 2:16). He believed the only way to enter a right relationship with God is through faith in Christ. This faith brings new life that the law or good works could not bring. Using Abraham as an example, Paul asserted that faith alone made one righteous in God's eyes. If this was so, then Gentiles as well as Jews had access to a relationship with God through faith. Through faith, the Gentiles became Abraham's descendants and inheritors of God's promises (see Romans).

Finally a conference was held with the leaders of the church in Jerusalem to decide by what means Gentiles might enter the faith community. James, Peter, and the others agreed that Gentiles must not be required to follow Jewish law in order to become Christians. However, they recommended that the Gentile Christians avoid idolatry, unchastity, and follow certain dietary restrictions. These regulations dealt with relationships between Jewish and Gentile Christians within the fellowship of the church. The idea was to make the presence of Gentile Christians at the common meal more acceptable to Jewish Christians who wanted to attend.

The problem of admitting Gentile Christians apparently vanished when the Jerusalem community scattered under persecutions. Paul did not introduce such regulations among the churches in Asia Minor. Paul's version of the Christian message of justification by faith is the one that swept the world.

Finally, through Christ, the Gentiles received the blessings promised when God said to Abraham, "All the Gentiles shall be blessed in you" (Galatians 3:8).

Talking With Children

It is hard to talk with children about words and actions that involve prejudice. Yet they often understand prejudice better than we may believe. Many children can pick up on prejudice expressed as you read a Bible passage to them. They can understand the idea that Gentiles were not well-liked, especially if you give a simple explanation: In the Old Testament Gentiles were the people who did not yet know God or follow God's ways. Yet God knew about the Gentiles. God planned for the Gentiles to become faithful followers of God. But in the Old Testament that hadn't yet happened.

In the New Testament passages children may become confused, since some passages show Gentiles in a favorable light while others give a negative connotation. You can explain that during New Testament times Jesus ministered to some people who did not yet know God. Through Jesus those people came to know and follow God. You can also explain that some of Jesus' followers went to people who did not know God. Those disciples told people about God and Jesus. When the people became followers of Jesus, it did not matter whether they had been called Jews or Gentiles. Now they were Christians because they wanted to follow Jesus. People in churches sometimes disagreed about the best way to follow God, just as Christians now disagree about the best way to follow God today.

Talking With Youth

To help youth understand more about the distinctions between Jews and Gentiles, they might make a comparison chart, showing some differences between the two groups. They might also examine some of the laws in the Old Testament about ritual purity, or "cleanliness" and "uncleanliness."

Youth might also examine attitudes about Gentiles in various parts of the Bible. They might compare attitudes about Gentiles to attitudes they or others have about persons who do not worship the same God as they do or who do not follow the same religious customs. You will probably need to help youth understand more about the contempt and fear that the Jews felt for Gentiles based on laws for ritual purity.

Because teens are often idealistic, they can identify with the biblical idea that God was seeking for all persons to follow God. Yet they can see how hard it is to suddenly erase all previous distinctions among groups. You might ask some of the following questions: Imagine that a person from your church went to the home of a non-Christian. The person told the story of Jesus to a group of non-Christians gathered in the home. The non-Christians said they had received God's blessings and asked to be baptized. What would you think about what was reported to have happened? What would people in your church do and say in response to the story? Would your church expect any proof of belief? Would the church expect the persons who had been non-believers to act in particular ways to prove they were now loyal to God?

Talking With Adults

Adults may already have some understanding of the term *Gentile*. They may understand that *Gentile* means a person who was not a Jew. To them the term *Gentile* may be simply a fact. However, they may not be familiar with the whole range of ideas that the Bible presents in connection with the term *Gentile*.

You can help adults to a greater understanding of the term *Gentile* by sharing information about the term and by helping adults examine some Bible passages. Adults may be familiar with many Bible passages that mention Gentiles, but they will understand more about the theme of Gentiles in the Bible if they can examine in one study several types of passages about Gentiles. It will also be helpful if they examine the same passages in several different translations of the Bible.

Help adults understand that the term *Gentile* was for a long time a curse, even though God had plans to bless the Gentiles. Help adults understand Paul's ideas that persons enter into a right relationship with God through faith, rather than through following certain rules. Help them examine their own ideas about what place religious rituals have in a believer's life if acceptance by God is based on faith.

Like the Jewish Christians of the early church, Christians today may find it hard to understand that persons who were at one time considered unacceptable to God's people are now to be accepted into the fellowship of Christians simply on the basis of their faith in Christ. You may want to have your class discuss some of these questions aloud. Or you may ask adults to examine their own ideas silently. What people do I consider cursed and separated from God? Why? Is it hard for me to accept certain people who profess faith in Christ? Do I believe that I am accepted by God for my faith, rather than for who I am or what I do?

Cheryl Reames is a free-lance writer living in Herndon, Virginia.

From Teacher in the Church Today, *January 1992; pages 18-21. Copyright © 1991 by Cokesbury.*

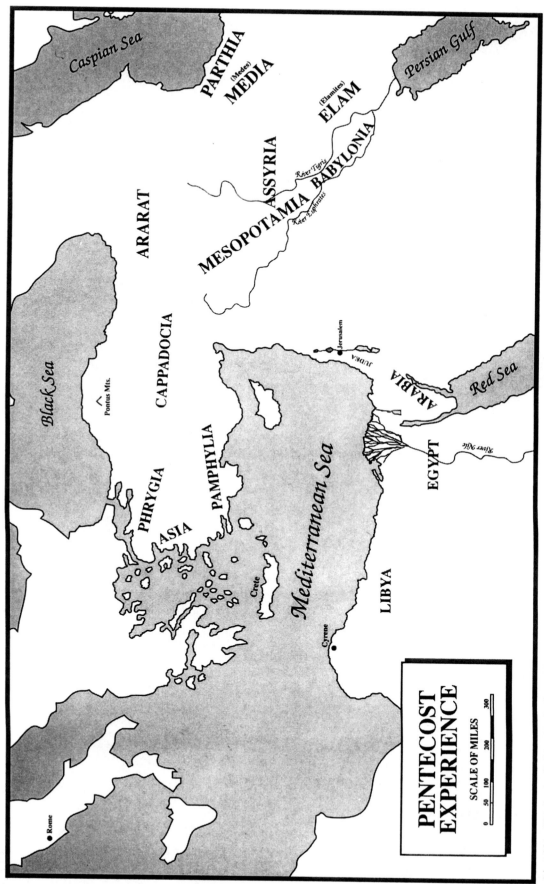

PENTECOST EXPERIENCE

SCALE OF MILES

0 50 100   200   300

Adapted from *Bible Teacher Kit* © by Abingdon Press. 1994.

CPSIA information can be obtained
at www.ICGtesting.com
Printed in the USA
FFOW01n1027160118
44582442-44435FF

9 781426 710292